SOUTH WALES BUSES
THE FIRST DECADE OF DEREGULATION

by

Andrew Wiltshire

The NBC-owned Western Welsh group of companies was a late convert to the Bristol VRT, not receiving its first examples until 1977. This batch, with ECW 74-seat bodywork and Leyland 501 engines, was numbered HR15-2477 (SKG 894-903S), the last four being allocated to Red and White. Following the creation of National Welsh on 27 April 1978, a further forty-six similar vehicles were purchased new in the years up to 1980, and included thirty with extra low-height bodywork. As mentioned elsewhere in this book, a number of more unusual second-hand Bristol VRTs were acquired between 1981 and 1983. These included nineteen Series-2 models from West Midlands PTE which had MCW bodywork to the standard PTE design. The subject of this photograph of 23 May 1991 is number 826 (OCY 913R), and is interesting in that it is one of three leased from South Wales Transport in 1986. The vehicle was based at Barry depot, and is seen at Barry Island while working a town service. The livery carried is that introduced in 1989, but has been spoilt by the addition of a large advertisement for local radio station Touch. OCY 913R ended its days working for Pratt of Quedgeley near Gloucester from June 1995.

(Andrew Wiltshire)

Introduction

The deregulation of bus services across the United Kingdom was to be the most dramatic change to the industry for many years. Only London would escape the events of 26 October 1986, as it would be dealt with at a later date. From this date we were to witness an "Indian summer" for many older buses as operators made their first foray into service work, while other operators were obviously not prepared for the new competition and struggled to come to terms with deregulation. Minibuses started to appear in significant numbers across the country from 1985, and these would play an important part in all the changes taking place.

This book does not set out to be a definitive record of the period, but more of an unashamed wallow in nostalgia, illustrating the variety of vehicle types chosen to provide services across South and West Wales. We begin in 1986 and gradually move forward to 1996 charting most of the major changes along the way. Many familiar names will be seen gracing the sides of buses in this book including a number of fleets featured in my earlier books *Municipal Buses of South Wales* and *Independent Buses of South and West Wales*. By the end of 1996 a significant list of operators had sold out or ceased to trade, and so this seems a good point to conclude our journey through the early years of deregulation. Where appropriate, I will briefly touch on the subsequent history of any operators that survived beyond 1996.

Acknowledgements

The original idea for this book was born a couple of years ago, and the project has gradually evolved over the past few months. With so much excellent material available it was always going to be difficult to select views and also establish a theme. During the compilation of the book, I have continued to learn a great deal about the events that occurred and changes that evolved in this area, since that landmark day in 1986.

A very large thank you must go to John Jones for his time and effort willingly given to researching matters relating to this project. John has also provided many of the superb images for inclusion which together with those from my father, John Wiltshire, and my own collection hopefully present a pleasing record of buses working in south and west Wales during the first decade of deregulation. My thanks also go out to Chris Aston at Omnicolour, and also to Cliff Essex, for supplying some excellent images. Finally many thanks to Vernon Morgan and Simon Nicholas for their valuable help with queries.

As always, thanks must go out to my friends and colleagues at the Wythall Transport Museum, for their continued support and interest in my publications. Written sources used throughout include copies of Ian Allan British Bus Fleets, Capital Transport and British Bus Publishing Bus Handbooks, PSV Circle fleet histories and a number of other publications.

Andrew Wiltshire - Cardiff, April 2012.

Published by Bernard McCall, 400 Nore Road, Portishead, Bristol, BS20 8EZ, England. Website : www.coastalshipping.co.uk. Telephone/fax : 01275 846178.
E-mail : bernard@coastalshipping.co.uk.
All distribution enquiries should be addressed to the publisher.

Printed by Amadeus Press, Ezra House, West 26 Business Park, Cleckheaton, West Yorkshire, BD19 4TQ. Telephone : 01274 863210; fax : 01274 863211.
E-mail : info@amadeuspress.co.uk; website : www.amadeuspress.co.uk

ISBN : 978-1-902953-57-1

Front cover: Cyril Evans was a very well-known coach operator from Senghenydd to the north-west of Caerphilly. Operations started just before World War 2 with a Bristol B from Aberdare UDC, which was put to work on mining contracts. Over the years, many coaches of Bedford manufacture were purchased before a gradual move to Leylands took place. Latterly based at Cwmparc Garage, the first move into stage services took place on 27 October 1986 with a route from Senghenydd to Caerphilly via Trecenydd. Gradually further services radiating from the Caerphilly area were introduced, including a joint operation with Red and White which saw Evans working the 50 from Bargoed to Newport via Caerphilly. Initially, grant-specification Leyland Leopards were used with an eventual move to Leyland Nationals and Metroriders. Slightly further afield, in this view we see former London Buses Leyland National, N11 (AYR 348T) leaving Taff Street, Pontypridd on 22 July 1992 and returning to Caerphilly. This service was introduced by early 1992 and the journey would take about thirty minutes. By this date, Cyril Evans was using seven former London Buses Leyland Nationals, and went on to have a fleet of fourteen, two of which had been fitted with Volvo engines. AYR 348T has two Mercedes-Benz minibuses from the Shamrock fleet for company in this view.

(John Jones)

Back cover: Between 1992 and 1997 Rhondda took delivery of nearly thirty new Dennis Darts with bodywork from Wright, Plaxton and Marshall, and in addition nine Plaxton-bodied Volvo B6s were purchased in 1994. Used saloons acquired provided a fascinating selection, with a number of Leyland Lynx joined by Tigers and Volvo B10Ms, some of which had received new bus bodies. In December 1995 two very smart Mercedes-Benz 0405 saloons with Optare Prisma 49-seat bodies entered service, and apparently, Rhondda Buses had an option on a further two similar buses, which alas they did not take up. The Optare Prisma incorporated a standard Mercedes-Benz front end and was therefore similar at first glance to the Wright-bodied version. The Prisma was not a common vehicle and only 121 were built with the largest customers being Grampian and Tees and District taking just over half those built. The Rhondda Bus livery suited its two examples 550 and 551 very well, as can be judged in this view of 550 passing Cardiff Castle on 20 July 1996. It is working the X8 to Maerdy, a fast service into Cardiff from the Rhondda, which used the A470 and avoided Rhydyfelin, Taffs Well, Tongwynlais and Whitchurch. Both Optare Prismas passed to Stagecoach Rhondda in 1997, and were finally retired by Stagecoach South Wales in 2010, and sold for scrap in 2011.

(John Jones)

We shall begin our journey north of Bridgend in the town of Maesteg during the summer of 1986. Like many valley towns, Maesteg was at this time witnessing the terminal decline of its coal mining industry. It had been for many years an area of great bus interest, being home to Llynfi Motors, and also to their bitter rivals A E & F R Brewer at nearby Caerau. Llynfi kept a smart fleet of buses and coaches, mainly Leylands, and here we see Leopard YSD 343L on 20 August 1986 opposite Maesteg bus station. It has an Alexander Y-type body and was new to Western SMT as a coach in 1973. Llynfi purchased this vehicle in 1984 from Highland Scottish, and it proved to be the last addition to this well-known fleet. Still retaining its coach-type seats, YSD 343L was regularly used as a service bus, as seen here, and also on contract work. On 11 July 1988 Llynfi would cease to trade, the business being acquired by United Welsh Services Ltd, and immediately wound up. Of the seventeen vehicles acquired from Llynfi, only six Leyland Leopard coaches were retained, and were licensed to the group's Brewers fleet. Neither of Llynfi's depots were acquired, though the travel agency shop in Talbot Street became part of the group's Travelwise chain.

(John Jones)

National Welsh had operated a handful of small buses for a number of years, but these were usually dedicated to special duties. The first deliveries during the "minibus era" of the mid to late 1980s were a batch of twenty-one Ford Transits in 1986, 16-seat van conversions carried out by Robin Hood. Further batches of minibuses delivered in 1986 comprised twenty-nine distinctive Iveco 49-series with 21-seat Robin Hood bodywork, and the first of what was to be a fleet of over 180 Freight Rover Sherpas, many with Carlyle bodies. We see two Sherpas in brand new condition at Aberdare depot on an overcast, but very significant day. It is Deregulation Day, Sunday 26 October 1986, and the events that would subsequently occur across the whole of the country would drastically change the bus industry as we knew it, and eventually led to the demise of National Welsh. These two Sherpas, numbers 57 and 58, are from a batch of nine with Dormobile 16-seat bodywork. They are turned out in the colourful Bustler livery which was adopted by National Welsh for its new minibus operations at this time. The company was sold to its management on 27 April 1987.

(John Jones)

Between 1964 and 1972 Merthyr Tydfil Corporation took a total of 42 East Lancs-bodied Leyland Leopards, although there were many differences between the various batches. The 1971 delivery comprised six vehicles numbered 174-179, these being 51-seat buses based on the PSU3A/2R chassis, and were some of the last Leopards fitted with Leyland 0.600 engines. Number 176 (GHB 176J) is seen on 25 February 1987 in the wintery rural setting of Pontsarn, in the foothills of the Brecknock Beacons, on its way to Pontsticill. The livery is that introduced in 1983, which in turn replaced the orange and white livery that first appeared in 1974. This bus was withdrawn from service in April 1987, with similar 1972-vintage Leopard number 183 (HHB 183K), being the last of the type, surviving until the end of operations in 1989. As for 176, it was to see further service from March 1988 with Walker and Gent of Acomb near York. Fortunately, 183 still survives to this day in preservation in South Wales, having spent its final years with Parfitt's Motor Services of Rhymney Bridge.

(John Jones)

J D Cleverly Ltd who traded as Capitol was based in Cwmbran and, during the 1980s, expanded rapidly throughout South Wales as it acquired a number of established operators. In the Swansea area the large fleet of Morris Bros was purchased in May 1984, and with it came a second depot in Cardiff with a sizeable allocation of vehicles. Following deregulation, a route branded as "City Triangle" was started., This operated around the Swansea suburbs including Landore, Morriston and Blaen-y-Maes. Seen in the city centre on 11 March 1987 is Leyland Panther UOU 417H fitted with a 52-seat Plaxton Derwent body. Along with UOU 418H, it was purchased from Cream Line of Tonmawr in 1987, both buses originally being new to King Alfred of Winchester in January 1970. The City Triangle operation was to cease on 17 December 1988, and UOU 417H eventually passed to the Friends of King Alfred Buses for preservation, and is now based back in the Winchester area.

(John Jones)

The last new double-deckers for South Wales Transport (SWT) were a batch of seven Leyland Olympians with standard NBC-specification 77-seat bodies from ECW. What was interesting though was the choice of engine, the Cummins L10 6-cylinder turbo-charged diesel, coupled to Voith transmission. Numbered 901 to 907, all were allocated to the Ravenhill depot in Swansea where they replaced a number of elderly second-hand VRTs of both NBC and West Midlands PTE origin. All seven entered service in September 1985, introducing a very distinctive sound to the Swansea area. Here we see

C907 FCY now numbered D907 approaching the Quadrant bus station in Swansea on 11 March 1987 wearing poppy red livery and displaying the Welsh translation of the South Wales fleet name. This entire batch of Olympians later gained SWT two-tone green livery from 1987 onwards, the last SWT bus in poppy red being Bristol VRT 967. South Wales Transport, together with the other two United Welsh group fleets passed to Badgerline Holdings on 12 February 1990, and the seven Olympians thus became part of the Badgerline Group for a number of years.

(John Jones)

Glyn Millington based at Cefn Cribwr had made his first foray into stage-carriage operation with a Bridgend to Porthcawl service in October 1986, but gave up after a year. A second attempt was made in 1991 with a similar service that ran between Bridgend and Porthcawl via Kenfig Hill, but that was also quite short-lived and passed to SWT in February 1992. A very smart Leyland Atlantean GBB 513K is seen pausing in Kenfig Hill on 18 April 1987 bound for Bridgend on the original service, which was numbered 262. Of interest on this vehicle are the large panoramic side windows, and the clear absence of an off-side staircase. The nearside staircase was a notable feature on a good number of double-deck buses delivered to Tyneside PTE and later Tyne and Wear PTE in the 1970s. GBB 513K had been delivered as Tyneside PTE number 677 in June 1972, and was one of a batch of twenty-five long-wheelbase Atlanteans. A number of these were later sold to the Isle of Man National Transport, with GBB 513K being shipped out in 1981, to become N874 MAN. It was later repatriated to mainland UK together with GBB 510K, and in 1986 both passed to Millington where they were primarily employed on schools work.

(John Wiltshire)

A E & F R Brewer was a very well respected operator based in the former mining community of Caerau to the north of Maesteg. Albert and Fred Brewer had started running a bus service between Caerau and Maesteg in 1921 and were still running several local services at the time of deregulation. The Brewer company had long favoured AECs and since 1954, the AEC Reliance had been the preferred vehicle for stage-carriage service and, after production of this model ceased in 1979, several used examples were acquired. Four AEC Swifts from Cardiff were to be the only rear-engine buses operated by Brewers and lasted around seven years. The Leyland Leopard then found some favour as a saloon, as a number of examples arrived from the Merthyr Tydfil fleet, while a pair of new Dennis Lancets also entered service in the early 1980s. A revised livery was introduced in the mid-1980s when the traditional cream was replaced by white. Only two saloons were added to the Brewers fleet after deregulation, and these introduced yet more variety, the ECW-bodied Bristol LHS. Registered JUG 352N and MUA 45P, they had been new to West Yorkshire PTE but arrived from Nottingham in early spring of 1987. MUA 45P is seen laying over at Maesteg on 18 April 1987 having only just entered service. Brewers ceased to trade on 8 January 1988, and the following day a new company, Helproute Ltd, took over thirty-four vehicles, retaining both Brewer's trading name and the depot at Caerau.

(John Wiltshire)

When Rhymney Valley District Council was formed in 1974, it soon standardised on the solid and reliable Leyland Leopard for its saloon requirements, unlike some of its municipal neighbours, which were buying rear-engine models such as the Leyland National. In most years, deliveries of Leopards to Rhymney Valley were split into two chassis lengths, 33 foot (PSU4) and 36 foot (PSU3), with the shorter variant being based at the former Gelligaer UDC depot at Tiryberth, the remainder going to Caerphilly. Bodywork was usually by East Lancs, but examples of Willowbrook and Duple's Dominant body could also be found. Inter Valley Link inherited no fewer than thirty-eight Leopards and all but four of them received the new IVL livery. 62 (PHB 362R) was one of three Duple Dominant-bodied PSU4D/2R models purchased in 1977, and is seen in Caerphilly on 9 May 1987. This bus was to find a new home with Rossendale Transport in 1989, and received a new East Lancs body in 1993.

(Andrew Wiltshire)

Merthyr Tydfil was to make some major changes to its fleet in early 1987. Delivery of a batch of twelve Leyland Lynx commenced in March shortly after MTT had introduced a striking new blue and white livery. Three new Leyland coaches mainly for private hire and holiday work were also received at this time. When still new, Lynx D106 NDW is seen in Cardiff's Central bus station early on 11 April 1987, having just worked in from Merthyr Tydfil on the service which dated back to 1930. The Leyland Lynx fleet, all of which were leased, went on to number eighteen buses, the final half dozen arriving between August 1987 and January 1989. The last three, 116 to 118, were fitted with Cummins engines in place of the Leyland TL11. On 22 April 1989 all the MTT drivers resigned to take up employment with National Welsh, and from Monday 24 April, Merthyr buses were driven by new or loaned drivers. The end came for MTT four months later. Merthyr's Lynx fleet, being very modern buses, soon found new homes across the UK. In 2011, the first of the batch, number 101 (D101 NDW), is believed to be in preservation.

(Andrew Wiltshire)

The number of Bristol REs eventually taken by Aberdare UDC/Cynon Valley BC was to total thirteen, with the final examples arriving in 1975 as some of the last REs to enter service on the UK mainland. The Leyland National then became the standard model for a number of years, and would be the council's last new full-size buses. All the REs were of the shorter RESL model, so the addition of a used 52-seat RELL model in 1987 was a bit of a surprise. Numbered 49, JEH 179K came from the Southend Transport fleet, but had started life in 1972 as a two-door bus with Potteries Motor Traction. On 12 June 1987, number 49 is seen wearing the livery introduced in 1986 by Geoffrey Hilditch, the then newly-appointed general manager at Cynon Valley. It was heading for Llwydcoed when photographed in Victoria Square, Aberdare. Unfortunately, JEH 179K was withdrawn from service in September 1988 as, following a breakdown at Abercynon, it sustained serious accident damage while being towed back to Aberdare.

(John Jones)

London Transport built up a fleet of ninety-five BL-class Bristol LH6Ls with ECW bodies between April 1976 and the summer of 1977, mainly to replace some of the ageing RF class AEC Regal IV saloons on suburban services around the capital. The Leyland National was considered too big for many of these routes and so the Bristol LH fitted the bill. They had seating for 39 and, unusually for the Bristol LH, were equipped with semi-automatic gearboxes making them more suitable for service in London, where drivers were not used to conventional manual gearboxes. The majority of the BL class was destined to have a short service life with London Transport, and sales began in earnest during 1982. Rhymney Valley DC took four examples in 1983 and numbered them 31 to 34. Number 31 (OJD 45R) became fleet number 12 in October 1986 and is seen negotiating Puzzle House Corner near Bargoed on 8 May 1987. All four of the ex London Bristol LHs would be sold later that month, passing to Trimdon Motor Services, which allocated them to their Tyne and Wear Omnibus fleet by August of that year.   OJD 45R later passed to Tally Ho! of Kingsbridge in Devon by 1990, and had been sold for preservation in South Wales by 2004.

(John Jones)

Hills of Tredegar was a major coach operator which also ran a fleet of about eight buses on a small network of routes for many years prior to deregulation. Service buses tended to be of Leyland manufacture and were normally purchased new. Leyland Tiger Cubs were once popular but had gradually been superseded by the Leopard, and in this view we see a 1973 Leopard with 47-seat Plaxton Derwent bodywork. A similar bus, GHB 20N, arrived in 1974 after which the choice of body shifted to the more modern-looking Duple Dominant. OWO 139M is seen on 26 May 1987 at Rhymney, bound for Tredegar on the service from Abertysswg. Unfortunately it was withdrawn from service in October 1989 after an accident. The Hills business passed to J D Cleverly of Cwmbran in November 1991 together with fourteen vehicles including four saloons. Hill's local bus services were subsequently taken over by Red and White.

(John Jones)

To the south of the Gwent town of Brynmawr is Nantyglo, then home to John Morgan who traded as John's Travel. This was a minor operator who, for a short time, ran a service from Brynmawr to Abertillery. A regular performer on this duty was MBX 361H, a quite late example of a Leyland Tiger Cub. Fitted with 45-seat Willowbrook bodywork, it had been new in 1969 to Rees and Williams of Tycroes. The bus was to pass to Thomas of Llangadog in 1984, and John Morgan acquired it from Briggs of Swansea in June 1986. Here we see it in Brynmawr bus station on a fine 25 May 1987. John's Travel operated a number of other service buses at this time including three former Merthyr Tydfil Leyland Leopards. MBX 361H was to leave this fleet a few months later in the August, passing to the Herefordshire bus dealer Wacton, and the following month finding a new lease of life in Martin Perry's bus fleet at Bromyard. Meanwhile John's Travel ceased to operate its bus service on 19 December 1988 when Glyn Williams registered the service.

(John Wiltshire)

The first fleet in Wales to receive an example of the new Leyland Lynx saloon was D Coaches of Morriston, which purchased one for its West Wales fleet based at Tycroes. It had a Leyland engine, seating for 51, and was delivered in early 1987. D32 MWN is displaying West Wales fleet names and sign-written advertising for D Coaches' Diamond Tours, when seen on 4 June 1987 leaving the Quadrant bus station in Swansea. It is operating the route for which it was principally purchased, the Swansea to Llandeilo service 103. Further Leyland Lynx would soon appear in South Wales with Merthyr Tydfil Transport and in 1989 with Cardiff Bus. D32 MWN would barely see four years service with D Coaches and would be sold in January 1991, passing to Scottish operator Whitelaw of Stonehouse in South Lanarkshire. By 1996 it was working for Citybus of Liverpool, and eventually ended up with Pilkingtons of Accrington in 2001 for spares, being towed away for scrap the following year.

(John Wiltshire)

Islwyn Borough Transport Ltd was the "arms length" company set up at deregulation, and was commonly known as IBT from that time. Leyland Leopards were purchased exclusively between 1968 and 1981, when conversion to one-man operation was completed. The next new buses, three East Lancs-bodied Leyland Tigers, arrived in 1985 numbered 41 to 43, followed in 1987 by similar 44 to 46. All had 47 dual-purpose type seats and the final trio also boasted rear luggage lockers. These new buses became regular performers on the long route from Tredegar to Cardiff via Blackwood and Caerphilly. Passing Cardiff Castle and heading for Tredegar on 21 May 1987, when still fairly new, is number 44 (D44 MBO). This bus sports both Leyland and Tiger badges and carries a further variation to the usual livery, namely a dark blue roof. Number 44 was withdrawn in 2003 and scrapped the following year. The Leyland Tiger continued to serve IBT until 2008, when number 42 was finally retired.

(John Jones)

The final deliveries to the erstwhile Rhymney Valley DC fleet were an impressive trio of long-wheelbase Leyland Olympian double-deckers with stylish East Lancs bodies and 78 coach-style seats. They entered service in September 1985 in a new livery and with Inter Valley Link fleet names. This style and title was adopted by Rhymney Valley in readiness for deregulation just over a year later. These were fine-looking buses and had a very impressive turn of speed, and would regularly be found at work on the jointly-operated Tredegar to Cardiff service as well as on private hire duties, and the short-lived London Express service. This view of 28 (C28 EUH) was taken mid-morning on 9 May 1987 as the bus arrives at the Kingsway, and bound for the central bus station, with part of Cardiff Castle visible beyond the red Fiat. When Inter Valley Link ceased to operate on 1 April 1989, all three of these buses briefly passed to G&G Coaches of Leamington Spa, with 28 and 29 finally settling down with Badgerline in September 1989 as their 5000/1. Following the absorption of Badgerline into First Group the two Olympians later passed to Durbins Coaches and then on to South Gloucestershire Bus and Coach. In 2011 it is thought that C29 EUH may still survive out of use with an operator in Cambridgeshire.

(Andrew Wiltshire)

Peter and Paul Jervis operated initially from a base on the Green Park Industrial Estate in Port Talbot and traded as Jervis Bros. They tended to operate smaller vehicles which included a pair of Ford A-series, one of which was new to Welsh municipal Colwyn Borough. Larger vehicles of note included a former Hants and Dorset Bristol RELL NLJ 828G, and a Leyland Royal Tiger Doyen coach. By August 1987 Jervis were operating a local service branded "Townrider" which ran from Toll Road, Margam to Baglan Moors passing through Port Talbot and Sandfields en route. Hard at work on this duty on 24 August 1987 is Seddon Pennine IV midi bus XDT 326M. Jervis had acquired this interesting little vehicle in November 1986 from a church in Gorseinon, and continued to run it until February 1988. It had started life in 1973 as one of five similar buses purchased by Doncaster Corporation for use on special services in that town, which included the Inner Circle linking Doncaster's railway station with its three main bus termini. Jervis Bros ceased to trade in April 1995. Subsequently, operations restarted with private hire and contracts, and Jervis Coaches are still around in 2012.

(John Jones)

In 1965, A T Jones commenced operating from Isfryn, near Login on the deeply rural Carmarthenshire/Pembrokeshire border. Having a family shareholding in the well-established Preselly Motors, gradually, over several years that operator's vehicles and services were absorbed into the business. Pioneer of Laugharne was acquired in 1980, and rural services continued to expand through to deregulation by which time operations served Haverfordwest, Carmarthen and Pendine. Two smart new buses were received in 1987, an Optare City Pacer midi bus and this rather interesting Scania K92CRB. Hitherto service buses had been a mixture of Bedfords and Leylands usually purchased second-hand. D727 GDE was delivered in March 1987 and had an East Lancs body with seating for 59. This impressive-looking bus was purchased for the 222 Carmarthen to Pendine service, and is seen waiting in Carmarthen bus station before setting off for the well-known coastal village on 12 June 1987. The 222 was lost to Badgerline subsidiary SWT in September 1990 and D727 GDE subsequently passed to a dealer in May 1991 in exchange for a Volvo coach. It was soon sold on to Leeds-based operator Rhodes Coaches of Yeadon, and later passed with the Rhodes business to Yorkshire Rider in 1994 as number 8600. After a spell with Bullock of Cheadle from 1996, D727 GDE is believed to have ended its days working on school contracts for an operator in the Scottish Highlands.

(Cliff Essex)

The Metrorider was launched by MCW at the 1986 Motor Show and was a purpose-built midi bus, intended to be a superior product to its van-based rivals at this time. It featured a Cummins B-series engine and Allison fully-automatic transmission. Of integral construction, the Metrorider was available in two lengths and Cardiff initially took thirty-six of the shorter 7-metre versions that were fitted out with 23 seats. The first batch of ten buses entered service in September 1987 numbered 120 to 129, and similar buses numbered up to 155 were to follow by November 1988. Some of them had dual-purpose type seating and luggage boots. Here we see number 123 leaving The Hayes in the centre of Cardiff and turning into Bridge Street, bound for Penarth (St Cyres) on service P2. The date is 26 September 1987 and the bus is brand new. This area of Cardiff has now changed beyond all recognition. The building immediately behind the bus has gone and the site now forms part of the new St Davids 2 shopping centre. The large clock behind the bus belonged to the legendary David Morgan department store which has since closed, but thankfully the clock survives. In 2012 the whole area is vehicle-free.

(John Wiiltshire)

17

In 1986 Silcox purchased four former National Bus Company Bristol VRTSLs with ECW bodywork. These included series-one model OCD 770G and two slightly newer series-two models, all from Southdown. The VRT seen here at Tenby on 14 March 1988 is WHN 411G, a series-one model, the first of a batch of twenty that began life with United Automobile Services in 1969. It had, however, spent a few years in the South Wales Transport fleet with sister bus WHN 419G, before passing to Silcox, who repainted it into a revised double-deck livery incorporating sloping stripes. Since the 1970s, double-deck operation was confined purely to schools and contract work and, by 1991, a total of nine VRTs had seen service with Silcox. There followed a handful of Leyland Atlanteans and a solitary Leyland Titan, before double-deck operation ceased altogether on 22 July 1998 after fifty-six years. The arrival of twenty former MoD Leyland Tigers played a major part in transforming the fleet at this time. Fortunately WHN 411G was purchased for preservation by enthusiasts in the north-east of England, as one of precious few series-one VRTs to survive.

(Andrew Wiltshire)

It is possible to trace the history of Silcox as far back as 1933 when the vehicles and services of J R Ford of Pembroke were acquired. Over the years Silcox has maintained a network of services in south Pembrokeshire and in particular around the Pembroke Dock and Tenby areas. Since the arrival of a new K5G in 1942, Silcox has often favoured the Bristol chassis, with many bought new in early post-war years, and during the 1970s ran a large fleet of LS and MW saloons. Double-deckers were always in the minority, but in 1976 the fleet still contained a pair of 1952/3 vintage KSW types, together with some early LD model Lodekkas that were new to Crosville in 1955. Silcox later purchased five of the later FLF forward-entrance Lodekkas including this former Hants and Dorset FLF6G dating from 1966. FLJ 154D joined the fleet in 1980, and is seen at Neyland on 14 March 1988 having just completed a morning school service, and would be parked up until required for the afternoon run. Behind the bus can be seen the River Cleddau and the road bridge which opened in 1975, replacing the Neyland to Pembroke Dock ferry. FLJ 154D was withdrawn in 1989, leaving 804 SHW as the last FLF in service.

(Andrew Wiltshire)

Morris Travel of Pencoed had been in business for many years, with its origins going back as far as 1920. However, stage-carriage operation was something which did not come about until 1985, when the business of John of Coity (Coity Motors) was purchased, along with a number of buses. These included a pair of former Midland Red Leopards with Willowbrook bodies, YHA 414J and CHA 424K. The former, a 53-seater new in 1971 is seen in Bridgend on 1 April 1988, while working a town service to Quarella Road in the Wildmill area of the town. Morris ran a number of local services at this time, the only out of town route being that to Coity. By 1988 vehicles were garaged at both the original site at Wellhouse Garage in Pencoed and at the Litchard Industrial Estate in Brackla. On 20 January 1992, Morris Travel's services passed to Brewers but operation continued with contract and coaching work, today trading as Pencoed Travel.

(John Jones)

Commencing PSV operations in 1974 with a minibus and based in Cwmfelinfach, Glyn Williams was eventually to move onto much bigger things. By 1982 when he moved operations to Cross Keys, the fleet of eight comprised much larger vehicles, and in 1983 a rare Ward Dalesman coach was added. The onset of deregulation witnessed the start of an hourly service from Blackwood to Newport which was soon increased to quarter hourly. In 1987, a pair of Gardner-engined Bristol RESLs was purchased from the neighbouring Inter Valley Link fleet, and these were soon joined by a host of Leyland Leopard saloons, some of which had received new bodies after a refurbishment. Entering Newport bus station on 14 May 1988, with the destination blind already set for the return journey, is former IVL number 61, GTX 361N on service 151. The REs were sold in July 1989 to Hylton Castle of East Boldon Colliery, County Durham, where they received their new owner's "Catch A Bus" livery.

(John Wiltshire)

With Helproute Ltd having taken over Brewer's vehicles and its depot on 8 January 1988 (see page 8 upper), associated South Wales Transport (SWT) had also registered a network of services around Maesteg at this time. SWT then took the Helproute vehicles on hire as Helproute had no operator licence, and operations began. SWT deregistered these services when Helproute gained its own operator's licence the following month, and started to operate using the buses it had hired to SWT. By May 1988 much of the former Brewer's stock had been replaced by second-hand Leopard coaches from SWT, Ribble and West Yorkshire. One of the former Brewer's buses is UPD 269X, a Dennis Lancet with 45-seat Wadham Stringer body dating from 1982. It was previously a Dennis demonstrator, and joined a similar, but longer bus MEP 970X, that Brewer's had bought new. We are outside Maesteg bus station in this view of UPD 269X taken on 20 May 1988, whilst parked behind in the bus station is the other Lancet, MEP 970X.

(John Wiltshire)

The Glyn Williams fleet was set to expand rapidly with deregulation, and a large number of used saloons entered the fleet from 1987. Following on from the two Bristol REs, 1988 would see the arrival of no fewer than ten Leyland Leopards with a mixture of bodywork, including three with newly-built Willowbrook Warrior bodies. Number 2 (SCP 342L) was one of five similar Leopards with Plaxton Derwent bodies that were purchased from Cooper of Stockton Heath near Warrington, and which had originally been new to Halifax Corporation. A further two similar buses came from Cooper's parent company Mayne of Clayton, Manchester, and were of West Yorkshire PTE origin. The Plaxton Derwent body styling of these seven buses varied, and as can be seen, SCP 342L featured a non-standard front and a much more attractive rounded rear roof dome. The year 1990 would see further Leopards arrive, but this time with Duple Dominant bodywork, and also the first of what was to be a large number of Leyland Nationals to be acquired. SCP 342L is seen outbound, passing through Newport town centre on 14 May 1988 and heading for Blackwood. This bus had been sold by 1992.

(John Wiltshire)

Hawkes of Waunarlwydd began operations in 1971 with Bedford coaches, from its original premises in nearby Gorseinon. The fleet continued to grow with many second-hand acquisitions, mainly coaches employed on private hire and contract work. The move to Waunarlwydd took place in the mid-1970s, and the first stage work came after deregulation in late 1987. This took the form of a service numbered 98 that ran into Swansea and branded as "City Connection". During the morning and evening peak periods it started from Penyrheol near Gorseinon but during the day commenced from Gorseinon bus station. Initially the service alternated via Glanmor Road, Sketty or Gorse Avenue, Townhill, until an understanding was reached with SWT. After this Hawkes followed the Sketty route only and SWT ran via Townhill. Two of the vehicles used were rather unusual Gardner-engined Seddon Pennine 7 chassis with manual gearboxes. They had typical and distinctive Scottish Bus Group style Alexander AY-series bodies seating 53, and both had been new in 1977 to Western SMT but had latterly seen service with Clydeside Scottish. One of these buses, NSJ 4R is seen on Kingsway in Swansea city centre on 11 May 1988 with just a handful of passengers. The 98 service passed with the Hawkes business to Veolia in 2006.

(John Jones)

Eynon's of Trimsaran, based in the former mining village near Llanelli, was a well-known and old established fleet that had been operating stage services in this area since at least 1922. Many interesting vehicles, including numerous double-deckers, had been used over the years, often on the tortuous route between Llanelli and Kidwelly which in later years reached Carmarthen. By the mid-1980s Leyland Atlanteans had returned to the double-deck fleet, although a handful of Leyland PD2s soldiered on a little longer. The Leyland Leopard was still a very trusted and reliable saloon, and Eynon's ran many of these over the years, including a number purchased new. The example in this view from 25 May 1988, UCK 500, had started out in the legendary Ribble fleet, but had come to Eynon's from Hills of Tredegar in 1987. It was one of a batch of fifty similar Marshall-bodied buses purchased by Ribble in 1964. Less than two weeks after this photograph was taken, Eynon's sold their business to Davies Bros Ltd of Pencader, and two months later had been fully absorbed into the Davies fleet. Eventually a new company, Davies Bros (Trimsaran) Ltd, was set up and by 1989, UCK 500, still based at Trimsaran, had been re-registered BDE 67B.

(John Jones)

The introduction by Willowbrook in 1987 of the Warrior service bus body was an example of excellent timing as this was a modern-looking bus body, suitable for mounting on either new or refurbished chassis. Following deregulation many operators would not be in a position to afford new vehicles, so the Warrior offered an attractive alternative. Most were built on refurbished Leyland Leopards, and a number were delivered to Welsh fleets including Glyn Williams, Silcox and Davies Bros, while Richards of Cardigan took one on a Bedford chassis. The bus in this view is seen in Carmarthen on 18 May 1988 and had been rebodied in March 1988 for Hills of Tredegar on one of their existing 1972-built PSU4B/4R Leopards, FWO 154L. However, they did not use the rebuilt bus, and the following month it passed to Davies Bros of Pencader where, for a very short while, it gained the registration 788 FBX, but by July it had become 5519 DD. In December 1994 it was down-seated from 47 to 45, and was eventually withdrawn in July 1997. In early 1998 it passed to an operator in Dumfries bearing the registration MCY 132L.

(John Jones)

Taff-Ely Transport Ltd was formerly known as Taff-Ely Borough Council and originally Pontypridd UDC. From 1983 Taff-Ely was to experience an increasing amount of competition from local operator Clayton Jones, and following deregulation, things got even worse. By 1988 this arms-length municipal fleet was in serious financial trouble. This view of Leyland National number 29 (CBO 29V) was taken in the bus station on 11 June 1988, by which time the fleet had reduced to just nineteen vehicles. Of these, five were Leyland Nationals, whilst the only other full-size buses were three Dennis Lancets of 1984 vintage. The Leyland National had been the favoured saloon between 1973 and 1980, during which time eighteen examples were received, numbers 27-29 being 1979 deliveries. Unfortunately number 27 was destroyed by fire on 25 August 1981 when just over two years old, whilst tackling the steep climb out of Pontypridd bound for Penycoedcae. A brief vehicle shortage in 1988 saw a number of Leyland Nationals hired in from the neighbouring fleets of Cardiff and Merthyr Tydfil. Upon the demise of Taff-Ely, number 29 was to see further service with National Welsh as N659.

(Andrew Wiltshire)

24

A few of the former municipal fleets in South Wales had a tradition of maintaining a small vehicle for special PSV-related duties. This was some time ahead of the large scale introduction of minibuses witnessed from the mid-1980s. Cynon Valley (formerly Aberdare UDC) had replaced a 1972 vintage Commer 15-seater in 1979 with a 27-seat Ford A0609 and this was joined in 1985 by a 25-seat Dodge 50 series. The first of a number of small buses for normal service work were five Freight Rover Sherpas in 1986, numbered 1 to 5. After this the Dodge-derived Renault S56 became popular with Cynon Valley which took four with rather angular East Lancs bodies in 1987 and ten with Northern Counties bodywork the following year. To this were added five further boxy East Lancs examples from Newport Transport in 1991. One of the more attractive Northern Counties-bodied versions with 25 seats is seen in Pontypridd bus station on 11 June 1988. Number 12 (E932 UBO) is working the service from Aberdare which was introduced in December 1987, and had a twenty minute headway, competing with National Welsh (eight buses per hour) and Clayton Jones' Drysilver operation, (two buses per hour).

(John Wiltshhre)

The stylish Optare City Pacer was a minibus introduced in 1985 and based on a Volkswagen LT55 van chassis. Somewhere in the region of 300 were produced by Optare until 1992, and supplied to a variety of operators both large and small. A few examples were to be found running in South Wales, and Taff-Ely Transport took seven fitted with 25 dual-purpose seats in September 1987. They were numbered 40 to 46, and were followed by number 47, in June 1988. These were stunning-looking buses, and from a passenger's perspective, they were light and airy and rode well. Number 46 is seen in action in Pontypridd on 17 August 1988 bound for Rhydyfelin sporting Taff-Ely's fleet colours of blue and cream and the Pacer brand name introduced on these buses. Number 47 differed from 41 to 46 in that it was blue and silver, and was acquired from dealer stock. The Taff-Ely undertaking was sold to National Welsh Omnibus Services on 5 September 1988, which also acquired most of the vehicles but not the depot at Glyntaff. Only City Pacers 46 and 47 passed to NWOS, and number 46 ended up operating in the Cambus fleet in Cambridgeshire, where it joined 40 to 45.

(Cliff Essex)

In December 1974 the Borough of Newport Transport withdrew from service its very last half-cab double-deckers, seven in all including number 178 (PDW 484). This was a Leyland PD2/40 with a rare 58-seat Longwell Green body, new in November 1958, and one of forty such vehicles received between 1958 and 1961. Most of these buses were scrapped, but 177 ended up being exported to the United States, while 178 passed to St Mary's Youth Club in Newport. This ensured its survival long enough to warrant preservation, and in February 1983 it was re-acquired by the Borough of Newport.

Restoration to full PSV status had been completed by July 1988, and the bus was put to work on a shuttle service between the town centre and Tredegar House, where the National Eisteddfod was taking place. An immaculate number 178 is seen here at Duffryn near Tredegar House on 30 July 1988. In 2011 this bus remains in the same fleet which is now restyled Newport Transport Ltd, and it is used for special duties, often attending vehicle rallies in the South Wales area.

(John Wiltshire)

The minibus revolution came to South Wales Transport on a big scale commencing in 1985. This NBC subsidiary chose the Mercedes-Benz L608D van-derived model, which were fitted out with 20-seat bodies by Robin Hood. The initial delivery was for fifteen vehicles followed by a further thirty eight in 1986, and they took fleet numbers 201 to 253. Here we see 241 (D241 LCY) at Limeslade near Mumbles Head on 29 October 1988, heading back to Swansea city centre. It has to be said that the roof-mounted advertisement boards do little to enhance its appearance. The next small vehicles for this fleet would be twenty-five MCW Metrorider midi buses in 1987 fitted, unusually, with manual gearboxes and which also featured advertising boards. Many more Mercedes-Benz including 609D and 709D models then followed, with bodies supplied by Reeve Burgess, Phoenix and again Robin Hood. This had taken the total Mercedes-Benz minibuses in the fleet by 1991 to over 150.

(John Wiltshire)

The first vehicles to be added to the fleet following the creation of Inter Valley Link in October 1986 were five rather elderly Leyland Leopards that had started life with Midland Red in 1974/75 period. They had Marshall bodies with 49 dual-purpose seats and were purchased from a dealer in a rather well-worn state in May 1987. They did, however, dovetail nicely into the fleet which was predominantly made up of Leopard saloons. They had more recently operated for Midland Red (North) and following a thorough overhaul they entered service as fleet numbers 1 to 5. Ironically the previous occupiers of these fleet numbers had been similar looking vehicles, though slightly older, and with Willowbrook bodywork. Here we see number 1 (SHA 639N) which had entered service in August 1987, on a bright and crisp 12 November 1988, passing through Pengam, several minutes after leaving Bargoed, on service 50. At this point Inter Valley Link had just under five months of operation ahead of it, before selling out to National Welsh.

(John Wiltshire)

Upon its formation in October 1986, the Inter Valley Link fleet, inherited from Rhymney Valley DC, contained no small vehicles at all. In fact IVL did not acquire any until the autumn of 1988 when a requirement for extra vehicles was identified. Seventeen short-wheelbase MCW Metroriders were delivered which introduced a smart light grey livery, enhanced by red and green stripes. Numbered 101 to 117, the first five seated 25 and had luggage boots while the remainder had 23 seats with luggage pens in the first nearside bay. They all carried the branding "Inter Valley Classic" and would be the only new vehicles delivered to this post-deregulation fleet. Inter Valley Link sold out to National Welsh on 21 March 1989 and ceased to operate on 1 April 1989. All seventeen Metroriders passed to National Welsh, taking fleet numbers 2101-17, and all were transferred to Merthyr from 5 June. This view of IVL number 113 was taken at Pengam on 12 October 1988, and this bus was to see further service with Rhondda Buses Ltd after National Welsh disappeared in 1992.

(John Wiltshire)

One of the buses acquired by National Welsh from Taff-Ely Transport with the take-over on 5 September 1988 was this Dennis Lancet with East Lancs bodywork. It was one of three similar buses new in 1984 and numbered 35 to 37 in the Taff-Ely fleet. A37 XBO was a 47-seat bus, and has now become NS497 in the National Welsh fleet, but this was amended to DS497 in late January 1989. It is seen freshly painted in the new National Welsh livery in Caerphilly, on a bright and cold 7 January 1989, heading for the bus station, having worked on the Pontypridd service. The destination blind has already been re-set for the return journey. Despite their relative youth, these buses had a short career with National Welsh and were withdrawn by February 1991 and stored. Rhondda Buses Ltd purchased them in May 1992, but by 1993 they had passed to Vanguard Coaches of Bedworth near Coventry, and by the following year, they were working for Midland Red South as 2035-7.

(John Wiltshire)

The last full-size buses purchased new by Cynon Valley were six Leyland Nationals in 1979. In all, nineteen of this type were acquired between 1975 and 1979, after further supplies of Bristol REs became unobtainable. Number 28 (UTX 728S) was one of six Leyland Nationals numbered 23 to 28 received in 1978, and which replaced AEC Reliance saloons. All were to run for the restyled Cynon Valley Transport following deregulation, and receive the new livery of green, cream and orange. Number 28 is seen in Cardiff Street, Aberdare, on 11 February 1989. Prior to deregulation, Cynon Valley buses did not operate outside the borough, but after this date they ventured as far as Pontypridd (see page 25 upper), and by 1991 started a service from Pontypridd to Glyncoch. Further new services were the run to Merthyr and Cardiff commencing in 1992. A number of the Leyland Nationals would not last long enough to witness the end of CVT operations but number 28 did so, and would eventually become Red and White 444 in 1992.

(Andrew Wiltshiire)

The Bristol VRT had failed to make a good impression with operators north of the border, and the Scottish Bus Group soon struck a deal with the National Bus Company which saw VRTs travelling south to new homes in exchange for Bristol FLFs. In a surprising move, Tayside Regional Council took twenty long-wheelbase VRTLLs with Alexander bodywork in 1976, and this was probably due to the difficulty obtaining Fleetlines at this time. However, these Bristols would have brief lives in Dundee, and the five with Leyland engines, OSR 206-210R passed to National Welsh in 1981. When originally built they had 83-seat dual-door bodies, but were rebuilt to single door layout with 87 seats before entering service with National Welsh. They were based at Chepstow throughout most of their lengthy career with National Welsh and later Red and White, and could be found working as far as Gloucester, Newport, Ross-on-Wye and Abergavenny. On 22 April 1989 we see XR862 (OSR 207R) climbing Moor Street in Chepstow, and carrying the new Red and White livery, which it has to be said, is a great improvement over the previous application of NBC poppy red, which did not suit these large buses.

(John Jones)

G D & R E Morgan traded as Atlas Coaches and was based at Kingsbridge in Gorseinon to the west of Swansea. They commenced operations in May 1986 and a stage service followed in June 1988, which ran from Gorseinon into the centre of Swansea. For this they purchased a rather smart pair of Bristol RELLs registered TDL 566/8K, which had been new to Southern Vectis as 866/8 in 1972. They wore what was in effect the poppy red and white version of the NBC dual-purpose livery, though these buses were from a green NBC fleet. Initially there were plans to connect at Gorseinon with Celtic Coaches (J D Martin), who would run through to Llanelli and Burry Port. However, Martin ceased to trade and this connection never materialised. Here we see TDL 566K laying over in Gorseinon bus station. After Atlas experienced difficulties with the operation of the service, it ceased in December 1988. TDL 566K was to pass to Hawkes of Waunarlwydd in March 1991 for further service including occasional use on their own Swansea route, and it is pleasing to record that in 2011, it still survives in preservation. Atlas also operated a number of coaches, mainly Bedfords, and it eventually ceased to trade in 1992.

(John Jones)

Merlyn's Coaches Ltd of Skewen near Neath was founded in 1952 by Merlyn Williams, and was to remain a very small operation until the mid-1970s. Lightweight vehicles such as Bedfords and Fords were the usual choice, but then a new Leyland Tiger coach joined the fleet in 1983. The first stage carriage service, a route between Neath and Birchgrove, was advertised to commence on 8 March 1987. One vehicle regularly used on this turn was this 1974 vintage AEC Reliance NPT 992M that was fitted with Plaxton Derwent bodywork with a useful 55-seat capacity. It had started life with Gillett Brothers of Quarrington Hill in County Durham, and is seen here in Neath bus station on a gloomy 24 March 1989. The other service bus in the fleet at this time was F999 PLA, a 25-seat Optare City Pacer, and later in 1989, a former Merthyr Leyland Leopard JUH 228W, joined the fleet followed by a MCW Metrorider. Merlyn's continued independently until June 2003, when a merger agreement was established with Pullman of Crofty. The bus service passed to First Cymru by April 2004.

(John Jones)

Edmunds Omnibus Services Ltd was based at Rassau Road Garage at Rassau just to the north of Ebbw Vale. Operations can be traced back to the late 1920s and the fleet always offered immense variety, with double-deckers featuring for a good number of years until the early 1980s. By 1989 the single-deck bus fleet consisted of around six Bristol RE saloons, four of which had started life with Bristol Omnibus Company. These were supplemented by a Bristol RELH and a Leyland Leopard, both with coach bodywork. This view of OAE 957M was taken in Ebbw Vale on 27 May 1989, by which time the service to Rassau was the subject of competition from National Welsh which was using Bustler minibuses. OAE 957M was a 1974-built RELL6L model, with a 50-seat ECW body and had previously been in the Badgerline fleet. Edmunds gave up its local stage-carriage work in August 1989, and finally ceased to trade altogether in 1994.

(John Jones)

The last buses delivered to Merthyr Tydfil Transport Ltd (MTT) were five MCW Metroriders. Four of them (501-4) entered service in January 1989 and were 23-seaters. The final example 505, was originally intended for SUT in Sheffield as F105 CWG, and joined Merthyr in February as F505 CBO and with 25 seats. They all carried the branding Trippa and would be the only midi buses to join the fleet in the post-deregulation years. Here we see 502 (F502 ANY) on 24 May 1989, having left the bus station and bound for Wellingtonia Close on the Gurnos Estate. MTT was purchased from the local authority in May 1989 by a consortium of three local operators, Parfitts of Rhymney Bridge, Cyril Evans of Senghenydd and Ian Evans of New Tredegar. However, almost immediately Parfitts and Cyril Evans pulled out and Clayton Jones stepped in to join Ian Evans. Intense competition continued from National Welsh, which saw the MTT operation closed down during August 1989. All vehicles were returned off lease or sold off, and the five Metroriders initially passed to the Oxford Bus Co.

(John Wiltshire)

Silverline was a new operator that began running buses in the Merthyr Tydfil and Brecon areas at the very start of deregulation. Its proprietor was Martin Howarth who had previously worked for Merthyr Tydfil Transport, and who successfully tendered for routes once in the hands of National Welsh and South Wales Transport. These included major routes serving Swansea, Brecon and Merthyr, and later a Merthyr to Abergavenny via Brecon service. Initially the fleet consisted of three new Optare City Pacers, but larger buses were soon needed and the Leyland Swift was chosen in 1988. The first pair had Wadham Stringer bodywork with seating for 37, while a third example, F339 SMD, seen here at Abergavenny on 28 May 1989, was bodied by Reeve Burgess and featured coach-type seating. 1989 also saw the arrival of a fourth Swift, when E961 PME arrived from Jersey Motor Transport, where its stay had been unusually short. Some of the last new vehicles purchased were of Dennis manufacture, a Javelin in 1993 and a Marshall- bodied Dennis Dart in February 1994. The final vehicle purchased was a Mercedes-Benz 811D in February 1996, registered N859 PDW. Operations ceased in February 1997, the Merthyr to Brecon and Brecon to Swansea services having passed to Stagecoach Red and White. Three buses were acquired by Sixty-Sixty Coaches, while the Dart passed Rhondda Buses.

(John Wiltshire)

Having placed six splendid Leyland Tigers in service between 1985 and 1987 (see page 14), Islwyn Borough Transport then rather surprisingly opted for a truck-type chassis, on which to base bodywork for a batch of six midi buses in 1987. The Dodge GO8 had a forward-mounted Perkins engine and apart from use as a lorry could sometimes be found as the basis for fire engines and horse boxes. IBT again turned to East Lancs to build bus bodywork that would seat 25 passengers in dual-purpose type seats. The result was a particularly odd looking and very basic vehicle, with a good number of entry steps and restricted access between the protruding engine compartment and the passenger saloon. It obviously met the regulations to achieve type approval and gain a certificate of initial fitness. IBT seemed to find them reliable, and they passed the ultimate test of being able to cope with Bargoed Hill. Number 52 (D410 NUH) is seen on 30 May 1989 and working service 7 from Blackwood to Pontypridd. It is climbing Cardiff Road from Trelewis into Treharris, and dominating the scene in the background is the railway yard of Deep Navigation Colliery, which is now a country park. Withdrawal of these buses commenced in 1994 with at least three finding new homes for further service, number 52 passing with 51 to Pete's Travel of West Bromwich.

(John Jones)

Davies Bros continued to operate a fleet of around thirty vehicles from the Trimsaran site after they had taken over the Eynon's business on 6 June 1988. There were around eight double-deckers, including this rather smart Daimler Fleetline that was new in 1974. This bus, number 213 (CWE 795N), is seen turning off the main B4308 in Trimsaran, close to the depot and yard on 20 September 1989 and had been purchased from Skill of Nottingham earlier in the year. Its two-door body is by ECW but to a more unusual style that was specified only by Colchester Borough Transport (on Atlantean chassis) and South Yorkshire PTE. This Daimler was one of fifty-five similar buses delivered to South Yorkshire between September 1974 and May 1975, and featured a Gardner 6LXB engine in place of the more usual 6LX. Double-deckers were by this time still occasionally used by Davies on stage carriage work, but by 1994, there were only two left in the fleet, one of which was CWE 795N.

(John Jones)

As mentioned earlier, coachbuilder Willowbrook of Loughborough introduced a new service-bus body, the Warrior, shortly after deregulation. LAL 746P was a Leyland Leopard PSU3C/4R that had started life with City of Nottingham in August 1975, and had been purchased by Thomas Bros. of Llangadog in 1982. It was unusual in that it originally had a Duple Dominant coach body shell fitted with 53 bus seats. In 1989 it was sent to Willowbrook to receive a new Warrior 47 seat body, and is seen here in Carmarthen, in typically smart condition, on 20 September 1989. It has left the bus station and is heading off for Llandovery on the service operated jointly with Davies Bros, and will pass both the Llandeilo and Llangadog depots en route. Of note is the Welsh title Brodyr Tomos on the offside of the bus. Following the death of Ieuan B Thomas in August 1990, his brother Gareth continued to run this fine fleet. The office address moved from Llangadog to Llandeilo and the new fleet title Thomas (Llandeilo) was adopted. The depots at Llangadog and Llandeilo are still both operational in 2011, but Thomas is no longer involved with stage carriage services, with school contracts and private hire the only source of income.

(John Jones)

During the mid-1970s a number of NBC subsidiaries received Leyland Nationals with coach specification seating. The Western Welsh group took thirty-seven in two batches in the years 1975/76. They were 11.3 metre models seating 48 and were distributed around a number of garages, and here we see Barry-based ND404 (KDW 350P) running along Tudor Street, Cardiff. This bus had started out in NBC local coach red and white livery, and initially allocated to the Red and White area fleet as ND475, later becoming ND4275. By the time this photograph was taken in July 1989, it was wearing a special dedicated livery for the express service from Llantwit Major to Cardiff via Cardiff Wales (Rhoose) airport. Despite having been working for the privatised National Welsh for over two years, and the introduction of a new livery, ND404 has only managed to benefit from the addition of new vinyl fleet names, and is looking rather down at heel. This bus was withdrawn in early 1992 passing to Cynon Valley Transport, and eventually ended its days working for London and Country.

(John Banks - Omnicolour)

The first full-size vehicles for Cardiff Bus after deregulation arrived in March 1989 in the form of ten Leyland Lynx numbered 231 to 240. The Lynx was a modern stylish bus and the Cardiff examples featured horizontal Cummins L10 engines, ZF fully-automatic gearboxes and introduced a new livery of white with a brown roof and orange skirt. Six of them were 51-seat buses, while the last four had 47 dual-purpose type seats and five-speed gearboxes. As well as routine service work, the dual-purpose examples 237-240, were intended for private hire, hence the improved seating and were also fitted with tachographs. They soon gained a reputation for a remarkable turn of speed, but for normal service use the fifth gear was isolated, and could be unlocked by the driver using a special key when used for private hire duties. All ten were pressed into service on cross-city routes 12 and 13 from Ely to Tremorfa, as well as making appearances on the City Circles routes 1 and 2. Here we see 240 (F240 CNY) on more mundane duties at University Hospital Wales, also known as Heath Hospital, on 6 September 1989. It is working the number 2 service, the anti-clockwise City Circle route, that was previously the domain of Leyland Nationals and prior to that the AEC Swifts. Lynx 240 survived for a short period in preservation, making a few rally appearances, but was scrapped in 2011.

(John Wiltshire)

The well-known and long established business of Jenkins of Skewen passed to Smith-Shearings of Wigan in December 1988. At this point many new coaches were drafted in to enhance the profitable tours side of the business. The bus fleet at takeover consisted of Bristol LHs and Ford saloons, all of NBC origin, but only five were to be given Shearings fleet numbers and placed in service. Four of them were ECW-bodied Bristol LH6Ls, like 72 (JHW 121P) seen here waiting in Neath bus station on a dismal 29 December 1989. It does however look very smart in Shearings livery as it waits to depart for Crymlyn Road in Skewen. It is believed stage services started in October 1989 and other routes operated were Neath to Swansea and Neath to the Fairyland Estate, which is situated between Neath and Tonna. Shearings are thought to have withdrawn from operating these services towards the end of 1991, as the buses were reported to have been taken to Wigan by December that year. All were sold by March 1992 and it is thought that the services then passed to Brian Isaac Coaches of Morriston shortly after. Finally, Shearings closed their coaching operation at Skewen in October 1995.

(John Jones)

S A Bebb of Llantwit Fardre had a history that could be traced as far back as 1924. Their main route was from Beddau to Pontypridd, but from 1975 the stage service part of the business was expanded, and in 1982 a new and significant service from Beddau to Cardiff commenced. Vehicles purchased from the mid-1980s for service bus work have included seven unusual Caetano-bodied Fiats, ten Optare City Pacers, six Optare StarRiders and some Freight Rover Sherpa minibuses, all of which have been kept only for two or three years. In January 1990, two Dennis Javelins with Duple 300 bus bodies were added to the fleet, and were the first full-size buses used on service for a number of years. Numbered G25/28 HDW they had 55 bus seats, and we see 28 leaving Pontypridd bus station on 31 March 1990 bound for Beddau. Both these vehicles were snapped up by Eastbourne Buses in 1991, and G25 HDW was still hard at work with Yeomans of Hereford in 2009.

(John Wiltshire)

When Parfitt's, Rhymney Bridge commenced stage services on 7 August 1989, the first type of service bus to appear in any numbers was the Bristol RE with ECW body, some already having been sourced locally. There were two from the erstwhile Inter Valley Link undertaking, one of which, NKG 246M, we see here on 22 February 1990. The bus is turning right from Gwaelodygarth into The Grove and is returning to Merthyr town centre from Galon Uchaf. NKG 246M was acquired from IVL in 1989 and was one of two former Gelligaer Bristol REs operated by Parfitt's until December 1991. They went on to acquire several more RE service buses including three RESLs from Cynon Valley and several former NBC RELLs and RELHs. Also of interest were a pair of RELH coaches with Plaxton bodies dating from 1971, and new to Thames Valley, which took the RE total up to 14. In updating the fleet, the Bristol RE was gradually replaced by Leyland Leopards, and finally, from 1991 onwards, by Leyland Nationals.

(John Jones)

Evans of New Tredegar began operations way back in 1922 when Thomas Evans started trading with a converted lorry. By the 1950s they were a well-known operator in South Wales involved with colliery and factory contracts, as well as excursion and private hire work. For many years Evans ran express services down into Cardiff for office workers. The business passed from Thomas to son Harold, and eventually by the late 1980s, grandson Ian was in charge. The first service buses for use on new Merthyr area routes arrived in November 1989 in the form of three Bristol RELLs. New to West Yorkshire Road Car, MWW 751K was one of a pair that came from Edmunds of Rassau; the other, DAO 295K, had been new to Cumberland M.S. The former is seen here in Merthyr town centre on 25 July 1990 while working a service to/from Dowlais under the "Tydfil Trotter" branding. The Evans business was by now beginning to founder, following the failure of the partnership with Clayton Jones, which had hoped to secure the MTT operation in August 1989. Evans of New Tredegar finally gave up its Merthyr services in February 1991. The buses were, however, retained for a number of years after this, with MWW 751K and DAO 295K passing to Peakbus of Derbyshire in 1995. Evans ceased to trade completely in 1996.

(John Jones)

It is fair to say that during its fourteen-year existence from 1978 to 1992, National Welsh tended to use a large proportion of its coaches as buses, and I think it is therefore correct to include an example here. There were large numbers of Leopards and Tigers and a few Bristol RELHs, and bodywork was usually by Plaxton or Duple, but there were interesting exceptions on Leopards such as Willowbrook and ECW bodies. In late 1982 National Welsh took delivery of its last new Leyland Leopards, and some of the last to enter service anywhere, a trio of 12 metre PSU5E/4R examples with 53-seat ECW B51-type bodies. They took fleet numbers UC8217-19 and were registered PKG 104-6Y though they were originally allocated X-suffix plates. They carried standard National Express white livery and were renumbered to UC193-5 in early 1983. By the late 1980s they had been drafted on to bus duties and the identities of these coaches changed on a number of occasions. By 1989 they were numbered UC893-5 with registrations AAX 528/62/63A, and subsequently losing the UC prefix. This is how we see 894 in Bridgend on 20 July 1990, in Swiftlink livery and working the X14 bound for Cardiff. 893 and 894 were later re-registered UDW 640/39Y.

(John Jones)

Golden Coaches was a newcomer to bus operation when it commenced trading in October 1988. It was founded by David Gee and was originally based in Aberdare, but soon moved to Llandow near Llantwit Major. A local service from Llantwit Major to St Athan was later extended to run through to Cardiff, and for this, a variety of vehicles, mainly buses were acquired over the next few years. The first bus was LTG 40L, a former Cynon Valley Bristol RESL, and this is seen in Cardiff bus station on a fine 24 July 1990. Other vehicles of note used on this service were a pair of former Premier Travel AEC Reliance coaches, an ex Yorkshire Rider Leyland Leopard and a Bristol VRT that was new to United Automobile. The service from Llantwit Major to Cardiff via Barry continued to operate until 15 February 1995 when it passed to Cardiff Bus. Included in the deal was the depot at Llandow but no vehicles. Cardiff then sold this operation on to Brewers on 1 October 1995, who were by this time, part of the First Bus group.

(Andrew Wiltshire)

By the late 1980s very few new double-deckers were to be found entering service with any operators in South and West Wales. Cardiff Bus received its last Leyland Olympians in 1986, and then concentrated on buying large numbers of Metrorider midi buses from MCW and later Optare, as well as several batches of Leyland Lynx (see page 37). It was therefore a pleasant surprise to see the arrival of seven Alexander-bodied Scania N113 double-deckers in July 1990. They had seating for 80 passengers and were purchased from a dealer as opposed to being built to order. These were to be the first of many Scanias purchased by Cardiff over the following twenty years, although most would be saloons. They entered service in August 1990 in a revised livery, which featured more white and a new style fleet name. Number 603 is seen at the terminus of the 65 in St Mellons very early on 30 August, when still new. Three similar buses were purchased in 1992, and were initially used on the Ebbw Vale Garden Festival service, and all ten were sold somewhat prematurely in 2000. Five passed to Stott's of Oldham while the remaining five, including 603, passed to NIBS of Wickford in Essex. Remarkably all ten were still running as such in 2011.

(Andrew Wiltshire)

Alongside the Bristol RE saloons Parfitt's ran eight Leyland Leopards with a mixture of Duple Dominant and East Lancs bus bodies. Four of these had come straight from the Merthyr Tydfil fleet including East Lancs-bodied HHB 183K, and three 33ft models with Duple bodies that had started life with Chester City Transport. A further pair, which had been new to Merthyr as JUH 227/9W, arrived from Cyril Evans of Senghenydd in 1990. The bus in this view also joined Parfitt's in 1990, and was of Scottish origin, having previously worked for Grahams Bus Service of Paisley, which had bought it new in 1979. It was, however, based on a longer, thirty-six foot PSU3E/4R chassis, and its Duple Dominant body had seating for 55. JYS 616T is seen at the Twynygarreg terminus high above Treharris on 29 August 1990, and about to return to Merthyr. This Leopard was destined to return to Scotland for further service when it was acquired by Ayrshire independent Keenan of Coalhall in 1994.

(John Jones)

The old established business of West Wales Motors Ltd of Tycroes passed to D Coaches of Morriston in January 1984. This was after both Rees and Williams (also of Tycroes), and Eynon's of Trimsaran had been unsuccessful in their bids. By 1987, nine services were operated and the fleet stood at around forty-six vehicles. In the summer of 1987 the business of Rees and Williams was acquired by D Coaches, and gradually changes were made which eventually saw the former Rees and Williams fleet totally integrated into that of West Wales Motors Ltd. A new "Rees & Williams West Wales" fleet name was introduced. The Leyland Leopard remained popular as the everyday service bus, enhanced by more unusual buses like the Leyland Lynx (see page 13 lower) and six Leyland Nationals, three of which came from the failed Merthyr Tydfil fleet. One of these is former MTT 213 (WWO 641T) which was new in 1978 and is seen in Ammanford on 14 November 1990.

(John Jones)

In November 1988 National Welsh acquired for its Caerphilly Buslink operation the yard at Bedwas that it had been sharing with Waddon's Coaches. National Welsh had maintained its competition in a number of areas including Caerphilly and the Rhymney Valley and in 1990 a new livery was chosen for the main fleet, but the Caerphilly Buslink operation remained in the red and yellow or red, yellow and white scheme. Only one double-decker was initially allocated to Bedwas and this vehicle, Bristol VRT LR716 (GTX 740W), is seen on a very wintry 2 February 1991 as it climbed the Station Hill in Bargoed. The railway station is to the left of the picture, and the bus is heading for Newport on service 49, and will travel via Ystrad Mynach and Caerphilly. LR716 was joined later in 1991 by LD713 (BUH 238V) and LD727 (GTX 751W), both of which had received coach-type seats. LR716 is one of thirty Bristol VRTs new in 1980 that featured extra-low-height 13ft 5in ECW bodywork, and were fitted with fully-automatic transmission. By 1991 the twenty W-registration examples would be split up and most would end up in the newly created Red and White fleet.

(John Jones)

By 1989 the Brewer's portion of the United Welsh group had received an influx of Leyland Leopard coaches from SWT, Ribble and West Yorkshire as well as a batch of eight new Mercedes 25-seat minibuses. On 1 January 1990, the three operating subsidiaries of United Welsh Services, namely Brewers, SWT and United Welsh Coaches were placed under the control of a holding company Vanguard PSV Holdings Ltd, and on 12 February all were then acquired by Badgerline Holdings Ltd. Brewers received a number of Leyland Nationals from the associated South Wales Transport fleet including three vehicles from the 1976-built JTH-P batch. This shot of JTH 768P was taken in Maesteg on 1 March 1991, and shows the latest two-tone blue and white livery derived from the livery on page 8 (upper). The bus has had a B-prefix added to its SWT fleet number. In 1992 Brewers acquired twenty-one buses for use on newly-registered services in the Bridgend and Maesteg areas that would compete with National Welsh. In the same year Brewer's address changed from Maesteg to Sandfields, Port Talbot when the SWT Sandfields depot passed to Brewers.

(John Jones)

Islwyn Borough Transport will always be remembered for its fleet of Leyland Leopards with BET style bodywork, supplied by Willowbrook except for the last half dozen which were bodied by Marshall. From 1981 until 1985, the entire fleet, which then stood at 30 vehicles, had become standardised on Leopard chassis and most were the shorter thirty-three foot PSU4 model, though nine thirty-six foot buses were purchased in 1971/72. Three Willowbrook 45-seaters arrived in August 1976 and typically taking the numbers of the buses they replaced, they were 2, 3 and 30 (NTX 576-8R). They put in sterling service with Islwyn BT, and number 30 is seen here at Ystrad Mynach on 16 February 1991 in its fifteenth year. From late 1979 the buses began to receive dark blue roofs though the livery carried by number 30 is the version introduced on the 1986 batch of Tigers and subsequently applied to a number of Leopards. Number 30 was eventually withdrawn in March 1995 after an accident, and had been scrapped within twelve months. Following the addition in 1987 of the Dodge midi buses, Islwyn went on to take some Sherpa minibuses and also three 1977 Leopards from the former IVL undertaking which introduced the Duple Dominant bus body to the IBT fleet. A move into coaching took place in 1988 while a number of Mercedes minibuses were added in the years up to 1995.

(John Jones)

During the 1960s and 1970s Thomas Motors of Barry had kept a single-deck bus for use on its service between Barry and Cardiff via Dinas Powys. Initially a Duple Midland-bodied Tiger Cub had been purchased new in 1959 and that was replaced in 1970 by a thirty-six foot Leopard with a Willowbrook body. However, this was sold in 1982, and coaches were then used on the service up until 1989. The first Leyland National, GHB 787N from National Welsh, arrived in July 1989 but, due to its poor condition, lasted only until the following March. It was followed by a pair purchased in 1989/90 from Bristol City Rider which were in much better condition, and a further example, of Eastern National origin, from Brewers in 1991. In total, seven Leyland Nationals were owned over a period of six years. JHU 850L began life as a dual-door example with Bristol Omnibus in 1973, and still retains evidence of its centre exit which has been partially panelled over. It is seen at Barry Island on 25 May 1991 with the fun fair standing in the background. In November 1991, the joint working with National Welsh on the Cardiff service ended, when Thomas registered some Barry local services. National Welsh then registered journeys on Thomas' timings on the Cardiff service, and Thomas increased its own frequency to hourly on this run. Thomas Motors eventually sold out to the Shamrock group in January 1996 after 83 years of operation.

(Andrew Wiltshire)

At deregulation, Richards Brothers remained the dominant bus and coach operator in north Pembrokeshire and south Cardiganshire, and its fleet of Bedford service buses still stood at around twenty-one vehicles. However, since 1983, other makes of coaches such as Volvo and DAF had started to appear, and when Dyfed County Council specified modern vehicles for its tendered services, Richards had little choice but to look for something different as Bedfords were no longer available. This they certainly did, when in 1990 they bought the first example of a DAF SB220/Optare Delta 49-seat saloon in the south of the principality, followed by the first Dennis Dart in 1991. Here we see that first Dart H158 HDE at Newport near Cardigan on 2 May 1991 working the lengthy route 412 from Cardigan to Haverfordwest via Fishguard. The notice in the windscreen informs us that this is a Dyfed County Council supported service. Richards went on to add further new or nearly new high quality service buses to its fleet, and Bedfords are now extinct in this fleet.

(John Jones)

By 1990 Cardiff City Transport's batch of twent-six Willowbrook-bodied Series-3 Bristol VRTs had all but disappeared from service, with only numbers 310, 318 and 319 surviving into 1991. By the end of this year, however, inroads would be made into the first of the seventy-one Alexander-bodied examples that had been delivered between 1978 and 1980. On 23 May 1991 we see number 330 (WTG 330T) in action at the junction of Pentrebane Road and Waterhall Road in Cardiff's western suburbs. The bus is working the cross-city route 62 which takes it from Pentrebane to St Mellons on the eastern extremities of the city. The livery carried is basically that adopted in 1972, and the only changes in nineteen years being the substitution of Cardiff Bus/ Bws Caerdydd fleet names in place of City of Cardiff/ Dinas Caerdydd and the application of the latest coat of arms. The "Pick an Orange" slogan seen here was adopted by Cardiff Bus just prior to deregulation. Number 330 was withdrawn by the end of 1996, and Cardiff's final Bristol VRTs bowed out in June 1999.

(John Wiltshire)

The Porthcawl Omnibus Company came into being just after the Second World War, when a number of small operators in the area came together. In 1959 the business was taken over by Kenfig Motors of Kenfig Hill though the Porthcawl town services continued to be licensed to Porthcawl Omnibus Company. In 1977, John Williams, a former POC driver acquired the Porthcawl-based operation which was then separate from Kenfig Motors. Town services continued along with a Porthcawl to Bridgend service and seasonal summer services to a nearby holiday camp. The fleet has always been varied and has included many Leyland Leopards. A small fleet of double-deckers was maintained which included a pair of former Nottingham Daimler Fleetlines, ETO 176/7L, which were nicknamed "Torvill" and "Dean". Following deregulation, these would occasionally appear on the stage services which were usually in the hands of saloons and coaches. ETO 176L is seen in Porthcawl on a sunny 25 September 1991, and is working the Town Link service to Bridgend. These buses had 77-seat Nottingham-style Willowbrook bodywork featuring a centre exit, and were purchased in August 1985.

(John Jones)

In 1989 National Welsh adopted a smart new livery of red and white with green bands and a bi-lingual fleet name incorporating a red dragon. It was applied to both single and double-deck buses with a variation for dual purpose vehicles, while minibuses remained in the yellow Bustler livery. A change to a simpler maroon and white livery took effect from 1991 which was obviously a lot faster and more economical to apply. We are at Pontypridd bus station on 24 August 1991 for this view of National Welsh Bristol HR828 (GHB 84W), one of three Bristol VRTs with East Lancs 76-seat bodywork acquired with the Inter Valley Link fleet in 1989. At this time it was allocated to the Porth depot and has acquired a Rhondda fleet name, and although standing out of service, it would be a regular performer on service 132 from Cardiff to Maerdy. This bus passed from National Welsh in February 1992 through a succession of owners, before settling down to work with Forrest of Bootle on Merseyside in July 1992. By 1997 it was working for Mercury Passenger Services, a subsidiary of Maidstone and District.

(John Jones)

Jones of Newchurch, trading in more recent times as Ffoshelig Motors, had been running passenger vehicles since 1927. The road haulage side of the business was abandoned in the early post-war years and a number of services local to Carmarthen were then maintained. The operating base was at Ffoshelig Garage near Newchurch, just to the north of Carmarthen. The advent of deregulation eventually saw Ffoshelig obtain a presence on Carmarthen town services, and in 1990 they won tenders for further stage services and school contracts. Always an immaculate fleet, the livery was to change from the familiar blue and primrose to cream with light brown relief in the 1980s. A number of Bedford service buses were succeeded by second-hand Bristol LHs and Leyland Leopard saloons. One of two Leopards to be found operating for Ffoshelig in 1991 was UKG 423S, seen parked at Ffoshelig Garage on 30 October. It had been purchased from Davies of Pencader the previous year, and was originally new to Rhymney Valley as number 23 in 1978. It has a 51-seat Willowbrook body that Inter Valley Link had refurbished in 1987/88.

(John Jones)

Pullman Coaches Ltd of Crofty near Swansea ran a service numbered 54 from Cwmrhydyceirw into the centre of Swansea. Coaches were often used on this service, but a 45-seat Marshall-bodied Leyland Leopard which Pullman had acquired in 1991 was also a regular performer. That bus was GAX 138W, and had been one of the final pair new to Islwyn Borough Transport in 1981. This view of it was taken towards the end of 1991, by which time the bus had received Pullman's smart brown and cream livery. GAX 138W was sold in 1999 to an operator at Cork in Ireland and was scrapped by 2008. From its base on the Penclawdd Industrial Estate, Pullman went on to purchase two further vehicles from Islwyn, a Leopard coach and a Freight Rover Sherpa minibus.

By the end of the decade the fleet had grown to around twenty vehicles and was set to expand further. A number of Mercedes-Benz minibuses were now operated followed by the addition of brand-new low-floor saloons to service Swansea Park and Ride contracts as well as tendered work on the Gower peninsula and elsewhere. The business of Merlyns of Skewen was merged with Pullman Coaches in 2003 but continued to operate as a separate entity. In 2006 Pullman was acquired by French-owned Veolia and became a part of Veolia Cymru, much of which came to a well-publicised end in 2011.

(John Jones collection)

Following the acquisition of Porthcawl Omnibus Co by John Williams, the two fleets were garaged and maintained at the same Old Station Lane premises in Porthcawl. Eventually, the maroon and white Williams livery was changed to maroon and beige as used by POC. A former WMPTE Bristol VRT was added to the fleet in 1989, while further Leopards followed including a 1975-built bus with an Alexander body coming from Western Scottish. By contrast, one of the few Bedfords in the fleet is seen at Bridgend on a bright and crisp 15 February 1992. JWO 47P was a YRQ model with a 45-seat Duple Dominant body that had been new to S A Bebb in 1975, but had joined the POC fleet from Merlyns of Skewen in 1986. It has been engaged on the Porthcawl to Bridgend Town-Link service and there is no shortage of information posted on the windscreens for the intending passenger. A further expansion of services included the X14 from Porthcawl to Cardiff via Bridgend which was up and running by early May 1992, and two rebodied Leyland Leopard buses were purchased in 1995. The stage services eventually passed to First Group fleet Brewers on 20 October 1996. The remainder of the POC/John Williams business, mainly coaches, continued until September 2001, when it is thought Mr Williams retired. As for JWO 47P, it was sold in April 1993, passing to E W Jones of Blaenau Ffestiniog.

(John Wiltshire)

On 3 January 1992 National Welsh went into receivership but continued to operate at Aberdare, Barry, Bedwas (Caerphilly), Merthyr Tydfil and Porth, hoping that the business could be sold as a going concern. The year 1992 was also to see the continued rise and ultimate demise of one of the remaining former municipal fleets. A consortium consisting of Drawlane (Midland Fox), Stevensons and Tellings Golden Miller purchased Aberdare, Porth and Merthyr Tydfil on 4 February, but immediately resold Aberdare and Merthyr operations to a new company called Offerdemo Ltd, whose directors were on the board at Cynon Valley Transport Ltd. The former National Welsh Aberdare depot and operations ceased immediately, but the Merthyr operations, based at rented premises, continued with a mixture of former National Welsh stock. The CVT legal address and discs were used and the name Merthyr Bus was applied to the vehicles. On 22 February 1992 we see Merthyr Bus (CVT) 708 (BUH 233V), a 1980 Bristol VRT with an ECW body, running into Merthyr Bus station on a local working. On 17 April 1992, CVT's Merthyr operations passed to Red and White, and on 4 August 1992 the remainder of Cynon Valley Transport's operations, based at Aberdare, also passed to Red and White.

(John Wiltshire)

Cardiff Bus went on to take further Leyland Lynx saloons in 1989 and 1990 and, by the autumn of 1991, was running forty-one examples which included a dozen of the Lynx 2 variety. Then, in 1992, it was announced that the Lynx would be discontinued and Cardiff would have to look elsewhere for further saloon deliveries. A batch of fourteen Scania N113CRB saloons was acquired from dealer stock, which was basically a longer version of the chassis under the double-deckers described on page 42. They featured Plaxton's latest style of full-size saloon, the Verde, which made much use of fibre-glass mouldings, and had seating for 51 passengers. All fourteen entered service in March 1992 and took fleet numbers 272 to 279 and 281 to 286. There was no 280 due to the unavailability of a matching registration. They were to be found initially concentrated on the Heath Hospital to Butetown and Grangetown routes, but soon appeared on most big-bus services. A brand new 273 (J273 UWO) is seen passing through the grounds of the hospital on 21 March 1992.

(John Wiltshire)

Gary Lane, a former bus driver, wanted to run his own buses, and in 1983 started a minibus operation based in Tredegar. Business expanded and before too long he was running full-size coaches, a fleet which at one time reached fourteen vehicles. Contract work including schools was undertaken as well as private hire and holidays. One of his first service buses was a Plaxton Derwent-bodied Ford R1014 that had started life with Maidstone and District. Between 1987 and 1992 Gary's also ran a former City of Oxford Bristol VRT, NUD 103L, which was unusual in having coach-type seating. Service bus work had started by 1990 with a number of routes in the Abergavenny area and, at one point briefly included a service to Swansea. For stage services a number of Leyland Nationals were owned including ODR 444S. This had been purchased from Bygone Buses in Kent in 1992, and was unusual in that it had been new to Devon Area Health Authority in April 1978, and originally had 60 seats. In this role it had been used for staff transport between hospital sites in Plymouth. It is seen at the Garden Festival site near Ebbw Vale on 3 June 1992, looking very smart.

(John Jones)

After the closure of the Bridgend depot and the sale of the Aberdare, Merthyr and Porth operations, what remained of National Welsh continued to operate from Barry depot, while attempts were made to find a buyer. It should be noted that Cardiff Bus was by now providing intense competition for National Welsh in its last stronghold. In May 1992 terms were agreed for an employee buy-out which would be in the name of The Barry Bus-Line Bus Co Ltd (t/a Barry Bus-Line and Bustler). In addition to the existing vehicles at Barry, ten Ford Transits were acquired in May to replace the original eleven Bustler Transits which had earlier passed to Rhondda Buses in the TGM deal. Things obviously did not go to plan, as after services on the evening of 7 August 1992, the Broad Street bus depot closed its doors for the last time, and National Welsh operations had finally come to an end. The final fleet had consisted of 25 minibuses, 6 single-deckers and 13 double-deckers. From this time forward Cardiff Bus continued to provide bus services in Barry, and in 2012 still maintains a large presence in the town. On 8 May 1992 on Holton Road, Barry, we see one of the acquired Transits 450 (C462 BHY) that came from Southern National but was new to Bristol Omnibus in 1985. It is being pursued by a Cardiff Bus Metrorider in direct competition on route B4.

(John Wiltshire)

Changes to the South Wales bus scene continued apace into 1991. On 1 February the five Red and White area and Gwent Valleys depots were split from National Welsh, and passed to the Western Travel Group as Red and White Services, with headquarters at Cwmbran. When Hills of Tredegar sold out in 1991, four of their saloons passed to Cleverly of Cwmbran, who did not retain them for long. Parfitt's Motor Services took Leyland Leopard RAX 804M which was originally a coach, and had received a new Plaxton Bustler bus body in 1988. In March 1992 Red and White took the three remaining buses, which included Duple Dominant-bodied Leyland Leopard 360 (GBO 246W), that we see turning into Dynevor Terrace at Nelson Square on 28 April 1992. It is working the X38 service from Bargoed to Cardiff and has a healthy load of passengers on board. The other former Hills buses were similar UDW 137S, and Plaxton Derwent-bodied PBO 674R. Their stay in the Red and White fleet was brief, and all three were sold by July 1993. They would all find new homes and 360 ended up working for Smalley of Heysham, Lancashire.

(John Jones)

Clayton Jones entered the bus business in 1980 with a minibus operation and began operating larger vehicles in 1983, when the company Drysilver Ltd was established. At about this time he also applied for licences to operate services in the Pontypridd area in competition with Taff-Ely. In 1986 Shamrock Private Hire (Newport) Ltd was acquired and maintained as a separate coaching subsidiary. Further services commenced, some in competition with National Welsh, in the Merthyr, Rhondda and Newport areas. The Drysilver company ceased in 1988, having been superseded by Celtic Connection Ltd and Rhondda Travel Ltd, and the Shamrock fleetname also appeared the same year. In 1990 Shamrock was awarded the contract to provide buses for South Glamorgan County Council's Countryride Village Bus Network in the Vale of Glamorgan. These services link small communities with Bridgend and Cowbridge. For this, five unusual CVE Omni midi buses were purchased, all being 23-seaters and new in 1989 as demonstrators. Cowbridge is the setting on 20 June 1992 as two of these buses G208 LHN and F976 WEF lay over in the small bus station. The CVE Omni was a striking looking minibus and a number were built with the huge destination screen as seen on F976 WEF on the right. It was a low-floor design, ideal for wheelchair access, and was aimed at the social services market, as well as for normal PSV use.

(John Wiltshire)

Harris Coaches (Pengam) Ltd of Fleur de Lis near Blackwood commenced stage carriage services for the very first time on 2 November 1988. Using a pair of Carlyle-bodied Sherpas fitted with Almex ticket machines, they began operating services from Aberbargoed to Blackwood, and Tiryberth to Blackwood. Primarily a coach operator, three former Rhymney Valley Leyland Leopard saloons were acquired in August 1989, while a sizeable fleet of Sherpas was built up between 1989 and 1992. A Leyland National was added in 1990, followed by a further pair in 1992, all being of London Buses origin. One of these buses, THX 161S, is seen on 13 June 1992 at Penpedairheol, an area referred to by locals as "Cascade". On 1 January 1991 a service from Bargoed to Ystrad Mynach via Gelligaer numbered C17 was started and extended south to Caerphilly in February 1992. Another service that ran from Bargoed to Ystrad Mynach via Cefn Hengoed was numbered C9 and also extended to Caerphilly at this time. Harris later went on to operate a number of Mercedes-Benz minibuses, MCW Metroriders and unusual Marshall midi buses. They are still operating in the same area using mainly Dennis Darts and Optare Solos, and in 2011 they acquired additional tendered work in the Tredegar area.

(John Jones)

As mentioned briefly on page 52, the National Welsh operations at Porth depot passed to a consortium on 4 February 1992. As 12 February dawned, all vehicles had received the Tellings Golden Miller, Cardiff legal address and were having Rhondda Bus fleet names applied. Shortly after, following the failure of a local management buyout, the National Welsh Bedwas operation was also purchased. Initially services were run by TGM, before Drawlane set up the new company Rhondda Buses Ltd which was then granted an operator's licence. The newly-formed Rhondda Bus soon set about converting many routes back to "big bus" operation, and started to take delivery of some new Dennis Darts from August 1992 onwards. The first of four with Wright Handybus bodywork is number 97 (K97 XNY) which is seen in brand new condition in Cardiff bus station on 3 August. Its journey to Church Village would take it via Whitchurch and through the villages of Pentyrch, Creigiau and Efail Isaf. A fifth Dart with a Plaxton Pointer body also arrived by the end of 1992. In addition to Dennis Darts, nine Volvo B6s arrived during 1994, the initial trio being 10-metre versions for Porth.

(Andrew Wiltshire)

For its double-deck requirements in the first half of the 1980s, Cardiff chose to dual source its vehicles. The front-engined Volvo Ailsa was chosen to be mated with Northern Counties bodywork for thirty-six buses, while initially a similar number of Leyland's new Olympian would be supplied with East Lancs bodies. A Leyland Titan ordered back in 1978 for evaluation eventually emerged in 1981 as Olympian 501, and the first two batches of mainstream Olympians (502-519), were very similar looking buses. They were delivered to Cardiff between January 1983 and February 1984, and the bus seen here, 517 (A517 VKG), was the last to arrive. Some eight years later, on 15 August 1992, and showing signs of some minor tree damage, number 517 has been captured on Llantrisant Road in Llandaff and bound for Radyr on the 33 service. This particular Olympian was to retain the livery in which we see it here for its entire service life with Cardiff. It was withdrawn and sold in January 1999, eventually entering service in Cardiff with Guide Friday as an open-topper. After several moves around the UK, in 2011 it could still be found at work, as an open-top sightseeing bus in York.

(Andrew Wiltshire)

Tellings Golden Miller (TGM) acquired five Bristol VRTs and nine ECW-bodied Olympians from National Welsh in February 1992, but only the Olympians and one VRT were to pass to the newly-formed Rhondda Buses in May 1992. Four of the Olympians, MUH 281/3/5/6X, were sold three months later when a pair of MCW Metrobuses arrived from Stevensons Bus Services of Uttoxeter. The double-deck fleet at Rhondda Bus was always small and by the end of 1992 consisted of five former National Welsh Leyland Olympians, a Bristol VRT and the two Metrobuses. The latter dated from 1981 and were new to South Yorkshire PTE. Here we see 862 (JHE 152W) on 10 October 1992, leaving Pontypridd bus station on the 132 bound for Maerdy, showing off the smart maroon and cream livery which had been adopted for Porth-based buses by this time. Three more used double-deckers were purchased in 1995, but the last of them were sold early in 1997.

(John Wiltshire)

Cyril Evans briefly used a pair of former Merthyr Tydfil Duple-bodied Leyland Leopard buses on its stage services, but these later passed to Parfitt's. A total of eighteen Leyland Leopard coaches, mainly of National Bus Company origin but featuring Duple, Plaxton and Willowbrook bodywork, provided the backbone to the new services until the first Leyland Nationals arrived. From the summer of 1992, a fleet of four MCW Metroriders from London Buses joined the Leyland Nationals, gradually replacing more Leopards. In addition, two rather elderly double-deckers, ULJ 253J and XRU 281K, regularly put in appearances in service. Both were former Bournemouth Transport Leyland Atlanteans with normal-height Alexander bodies, and here we see ULJ 253J leaving Caerphilly bus station bound for Pontypridd on 29 August 1992. On 14 May 1993 all of Cyril Evans' stage services were acquired by Rhondda Buses Ltd together with a good number of Evans' buses including Metroriders and Leyland Nationals. Cyril Evans continued to trade as a coaching operation until December 1998.

(John Wiltshire)

Burrows of Ogmore Vale entered the coach business just after the Second World War and continued purely as a coaching operation until 1976. By the 1970s it had become necessary to bus school children from many of the South Wales valley communities, over some considerable distance, to a number of the new comprehensive schools. At this point the first of a number of double-deckers and a handful of saloons arrived for contract work and principally schools duties. Amongst these buses were several Leyland Panthers and a number of Atlanteans from sources such as Greater Manchester PTE and Bournemouth Transport. Burrows did not enter the stage carriage business until 1991, and in April that year they registered a service from Nantymoel situated at the head of the Ogmore Valley, through to Bridgend, passing through Ogmore Vale, Blackmill and Sarn en route. NNN 6M was a splendid dual-purpose Bristol RELH that started life with East Midland in 1974, and was purchased from Tenby Bus and Coach in 1991. It is seen on 22 September 1992, pulling out of Walters Road, Ogmore Vale, onto the A4061, and heading for Bridgend on service B2. This service later became half-hourly with alternate journeys serving the main A4061 road and Caedu, and was given route numbers B1 and B2 respectively.

(John Jones)

South Wales Transport was an early user of Leyland Nationals when it placed twenty-eight in service in 1973, numbered 701 to 728. Most of these were based in the Swansea and Llanelli areas, but further batches in the years 1974 to 1979 saw the type distributed amongst most of SWT's depots, Haverfordwest being an exception. In all, 115 Series-1 Leyland Nationals, all with seating for 52 passengers, were delivered new to South Wales Transport, enhanced by an additional eight used examples from East Kent in 1980 and half a dozen from London Country in 1982. This view taken on a fine 21 April 1993 shows two late examples wearing the post-privatisation predominantly green livery, and departing Neath Victoria Gardens bus station. Number 806 (WWN 806T) is working service 158 from Banwen to Swansea, and is being followed by similar vehicle number 814. The Leyland National 2 model followed in 1979, but South Wales Transport took only six of this type.

(John Jones)

The ruins of Newport Castle which are believed to date from the 14th century, lie on the west bank of the River Usk, close to the centre of Newport. They stand amidst busy road and rail infrastructure and in 2011 are no longer open to the public. With the remains of the castle in the background, the photographer has captured Newport Transport Scania number 42 on 19 March 1993. It is one of six N113DRB models delivered new in 1988, and followed by a further six twelve months later, all with 78-seat bodywork by Alexander, to their RH design. In 1993 the Newport fleet still featured a large number of Scanias, to meet the need for full-size buses, although from 1993 there would be a move away from double-deckers for a number of years. Scania 42 was to be withdrawn from service with Newport in March 2004, and sold to Northern Blue of Burnley, which later became Transdev Northern Blue. It was sold for scrap in 2009 following an accident. Interestingly similar bus 41 remains based at Newport Transport, and since 2004 has been an open-top sightseeing bus, serving the city in the summer months.

(John Jones)

Under the ownership of Western Travel Ltd since 1991, Red and White was now in the same group as Midland Red (South) and the Cheltenham and Gloucester fleets, the latter being made up of four units. At this point the livery was modified with the application of grey bands and a traditional scroll type fleet name. The fleet was very mixed with a large number of minibuses, including Transits, Sherpas, Renault-Dodge and Mercedes. Saloons consisted of Leyland Nationals, and coach-seated Leopards and Tigers. An effort was made to standardise gradually on the Mercedes for minibus work, while the saloon fleet was enhanced by further Leyland Nationals inherited from Cynon Valley and also purchased from a number of sources including City Line and Go Ahead Northern. One such acquisition is former City Line 660 (XVV 540S) which is seen heading for the bus station in Pontypridd on 14 August 1993. It has just crossed the River Taff adjacent to the "old bridge" and is passing the junction with Taff Street. The immaculately turned out number 660 will travel onward to Cardiff on the X78 service which originated in Merthyr. On 10 December 1993 the Western Travel Group passed to Stagecoach Holdings and so with it went Red and White.

(John Jones)

Parfitt's Motor Services ran this rather unusual Renault PR100.2 service bus between April 1993 and April 1994. It was one of only five of this type to see service in the UK, although the PR100 was a popular choice and successful vehicle in France. It was available between 1985 and 1994 and was supplied for bodying with a standard Renault R312 type front end. G276 VML was new in November 1989 and entered service with London Buses as their RN1 and saw service in the East London and Leaside Buses fleets. It had a Northern Counties body and originally had seating for 51 which had been reduced to 48 by the time it had reached Parfitt's. After service in South Wales, this rare vehicle passed to Hornsby Travel of Ashby near Scunthorpe, which was already successfully operating similar F100 AKB of 1988. This bus is believed to survive in preservation, but the example that Parfitt's operated was thought to have been scrapped some time around 2003. G276 VML is seen in Merthyr bus station on 12 July 1993 and about to work service P3 to Bargoed via Tirphil.

(Cliff Essex)

Clayton Jones experienced operating difficulties during 1989, and so his wife Alison obtained an operator licence and took over running the fleet in 1990. The Mercedes-Benz had always been the preferred choice as a minibus and many new examples were bought in the 1980s and 1990s. Early examples obtained for stage services were of the L608D model with bodywork completed by a number of suppliers including PMT, and with seating for around 20. The Optare StarRider based on the Mercedes-Benz 811D was tried, but it was the 811D with the Reeves Burgess and later Dormobile body that was to appear in greater numbers in the years up to 1993. The livery adopted for the bus fleet changed from all-over white to white and yellow in 1992, with the arrival of new K-registration Mercedes-Benz for the X6 service. The "Shamrock Shoppa" fleet name was still retained as can be clearly seen in this view of L468 XNR at Pontypridd bus station on 11 September 1993. The bus is working to Aberdare with a healthy complement of passengers, and is one of a batch of ten Mercedes-Benz 811Ds with Dormobile Routemaker 33-seat bodies delivered new to Shamrock that year.

(John Jones)

Cardiff Bluebird was the second operator to compete with Cardiff City Transport in the capital, the first being C K Coaches some twelve years earlier. Cardiff Bluebird was owned by Tellings Golden Miller, which had on 1 January 1991 acquired Cardiff-based Globeheath Ltd. Globeheath's vehicles were transferred to Telling Golden Miller's operating licence, and a new base was established at Penarth Road in Cardiff. Stage services commenced on 20 September 1993 with routes from Cardiff City centre to Ely numbered 217 and 218. The initial fleet consisted of Leyland Atlanteans from a number of sources, including three from Ribble that had started life with Greater Manchester PTE. One of these, LJA 641P, is seen in Ely near the terminus on 25 September 1993, its Northern Counties body dating from 1975. It is clearly showing signs of the Stagecoach livery design it carried in its later Ribble days. Smaller vehicles were also added to the fleet from 1993, with early arrivals being MCW Metroriders from London Buses and East Midland.

(John Jones)

South Wales Transport built up a fleet of ninety-one new ECW-bodied Bristol VRT double-deckers between 1976 and 1980. These all featured Leyland engines and were based at most garages, and two were re-bodied by ECW in 1981 and 1983 following mishaps. Withdrawals of earlier examples commenced from September 1986 with the introduction of a large fleet of minibuses (see page 27). A reasonable number were to turn up in other privatised former NBC fleets, such as Eastern National, East Midland and Western National, and some of these would soon have their Leyland power unit replaced by a more reliable Gardner engine. By early 1992, and now under Badgerline ownership, SWT still maintained a fleet of around thirty VRTs, one of which was an open-topper, and the last examples (992 and 994) were not phased out until March 2002. The introduction of the green SWT livery certainly brightened up the appearance of these buses, but sadly this example 992 (EWN 992W) is looking a little down at heel in February 1994 as it makes a final dash for Swansea's Quadrant bus station.

(Cliff Essex)

Parfitt's Motor Services had a requirement for a number of smaller vehicles, and a total of ten former London Buses, 25-seat MCW Metroriders was eventually operated, with most arriving in 1992/93. Two of these were obtained from the Cyril Evans business including E124 KYW which arrived at Rhymney Bridge in December 1992. Three of the Metroriders had coach-type seating, but E124 KYW had 25 bus seats, as can be clearly seen in this view taken on 9 February 1994 during the morning rush-hour on High Street, Dowlais Top. The lack of passengers and the "off-route" destination suggest that this is a staff bus working between Merthyr Bus Station and Rhymney Bridge depot. The following minibus is Red and White 300 (H370 PNY), a Carlyle-bodied Iveco Daily that was acquired with the Cynon Valley Transport business in 1992, and Red and White's only Iveco. Five Metroriders would still be on fleet strength when Parfitt's Motor Services came to an end in April 1995. E124 KYW was sold in January 1995 to Scottish operator Wilson of Carnwath.

(Cliff Essex)

Henley's have been running local services in the Abertillery area since 1950 and continue to do so in 2012. Never a large fleet, with no more than about five buses and half a dozen coaches, AEC was a favoured chassis type for many years. In 1987 the fleet could still boast two AEC Reliance service buses which operated alongside a trio of Alexander Y-type Leyland Leopards of Scottish origin. One of the AEC Reliances was WKG 287, a remarkable Willowbrook-bodied survivor from 1961. It had been purchased by Henley's in 1975 from Humphries of Bridgend, and had originally been new to Western Welsh. When new it had coach type seats but Henley's had fitted forty-one bus seats in about 1983. In this view we see WKG 287 about to pass the fire station on Castle Street, Abertillery, on 11 February 1994, with Henley's Leyland-Daf 400 minibus K151 XUK in the background. The Reliance was withdrawn in November 1996 after being slightly damaged in a fire at Henley's premises, and was sold for preservation during 1997. Unfortunately WKG 287 was broken up in September 2011. The small town of Abertillery is situated on the side of a steep valley, and the town centre makes for very interesting operating terrain for large buses such as this. It is well worth a visit if you are in the area.

(Cliff Essex)

Phil Anslow had been a coal miner before becoming a fitter with Varteg Motors. In 1984 he started a minibus operation and in the following years acquired two smaller local operators. Stage services, including some tendered, commenced in 1986/87 mainly in the Pontypool area, and some of which competed with the established operator, National Welsh. Vehicles initially used for the stage services were a variety of minibuses including a large number of Freight Rover Sherpas and a couple of stylish Optare City Pacers previously in the Bebb fleet. A small number of full-size coaches were operated as well as a former Islwyn BT Leopard saloon. By 1993 the fleet had grown considerably and included a pair of Leyland Nationals but these had gone by 1994. Four rather elderly Bristol REs had been sourced from Badgerline and smartly turned out in Phil Anslow Travel livery is DAE 511K, a 50-seat bus of 1972 vintage, seen at Varteg Hill on 20 April 1994. The REs were used on both stage service and schools work, and one could often be found running on the Tuesdays only Blaenavon to Abergavenny market day working.

(John Jones)

Bebb Travel of Llantwit Fardre pursued a policy of renewing vehicles, both buses and coaches, after only a short working life. Prior to deregulation, Bebb had relied heavily on grant-specification coaches for service bus work. It then switched to using proper buses and, following on from the pair of Dennis Javelins mentioned on page 38, were further Sherpas, another Optare StarRider and a pair of Carlyle-bodied 25-seat Fiat-Iveco minibuses. A return to larger buses in 1994 saw the arrival of six Volvo B6R rear-engined midi buses. They had distinctive Marshall bodies fitted out with 36 dual-purpose type seats. They were registered L81-86 CNY and they were to be the first Welsh examples of the B6 to be completed as buses. The B6 was launched as Volvo's answer to the Dennis Dart, which by 1994 had firmly established itself as a very affordable and reliable workhorse. The B6 was unfortunately plagued by teething problems, and Bebb's examples were no exception. However, when they were sold after barely two years service, all rapidly found new owners prepared to give them a try. On the afternoon of 14 July 1994, L85 CNY is seen turning into the bus station in Pontypridd. The building behind the bus is the Pontypridd Museum which was built in 1861 as Tabernacle Chapel, and also clearly visible in the distance is the "old bridge" dating from 1755.

(John Jones)

From 1992 Brewers concentrated operations on a triangular area taking in Maesteg, Bridgend and Port Talbot, and integrating services which had formerly competed with National Welsh in the Bridgend area. A new red, white and yellow livery was adopted at this time, and the fleet continued to grow with new deliveries and other vehicles transferred from the SWT fleet. The United Welsh Coaches operation was wound up as a separate company in September 1992 and the coach fleet passed to Brewers. Five Leyland Lynx 2 single-deckers were delivered that year, two of which were previously Volvo-powered demonstrators, and all five were initially dedicated to the Bridgend-Maesteg-Cymmer service 32. The bus here is number 510 (K10 BMS), one of the three with Cummins engines and seating for 47 passengers and is seen turning into Wyndham Street in Bridgend on 31 May 1994, complete with Badgerline logo. At a later date they were renumbered, K10 BMS becoming number 840. In the spring of 2001, two of the five Lynx 2s were transferred to First Western National for use in the Plymouth area. A further pair followed in 2003, but all were subsequently scrapped.

(John Jones)

By 1994, South Wales Transport was a subsidiary of Badgerline Holdings and many of its vehicles sported the Badger motif behind the rear wheels. This shot of Dennis Dart number 533 (L533 JEP) was taken at the junction of Kingsway and Dillwyn Street in Swansea city centre on 13 August 1994 and confirms that the City Mini branding, as used on the first Mercedes-Benz shortly after deregulation, was still in use to promote certain services. SWT took delivery of two dozen of these Darts with Plaxton Pointer 31-seat bodies in 1993, and had a further twenty-six on order for delivery in 1994. Badgerline, continuing its policy of major fleet renewals, ensured that the associated Brewers fleet also received some similar, but slightly longer buses at around this time. In 1995 SWT went on to receive further sizeable batches of Darts, but by now parent company Badgerline had been merged into the newly-created First Group. The first low-floor examples of Dennis Darts arrived with SWT in 1996.

(John Jones)

After building up a large fleet of Mercedes-Benz minibuses, by 1993 it was becoming apparent that larger and more comfortable vehicles would be required for some of Shamrock's services, in particular the longer routes including those into Cardiff. The first of what would eventually become a large fleet of 9.8 metre long Dennis Darts began to appear in 1994. The first six had Plaxton Pointer bodies, while subsequent batches featured Northern Counties and Marshall bodywork, all being 40-seaters. A solitary Dart with an Alexander Dash body arrived in late 1996, just falling within the scope of this book, and all subsequent new Darts would then be of the SLF low-floor variety. M425 JNY is one of the original half dozen with Plaxton Pointer bodywork, and is seen when almost new in October 1994. It is on Llantrisant Road near Capel Llanilltern and is heading into Cardiff whilst working the service 249 from Pencoed.

(John Jones)

Silcox Coaches of Pembroke Dock frequently purchased new saloons until 1980 when an impressive 63-seat Leyland Leopard with Duple Dominant body, BDE 140V, was delivered. There followed a period when large numbers of used saloons were acquired, and from 1988 a number of new Mercedes-Benz minibuses arrived for service bus work. In August 1994 Silcox purchased a solitary 9.8 metre Dennis Dart M174 BDE, with a rather unattractive East Lancs 40-seat body, which was sold after only a short time. Far more successful and better looking were three select-registered 9-metre Darts with Marshall bodies which were delivered three months later. They were well finished with dual-purpose seating, and were to be regular performers on the long Haverfordwest to Tenby and Tenby to Carmarthen services in their early years. Carmarthen is the setting for this rather nice view of M17 SMC taken on 14 June 1995. M17 SMC was still in service with Silcox in 2011.

(John Jones)

The Leyland National was to be Parfitt's preferred type of second-hand saloon from 1991 until 1995 and thirty-two Series-1 models were acquired, thirty of which were of London Buses origin. Not all of these would be operated, as three were used for spares. AYR 329T was rebuilt by East Lancs into a Leyland National Greenway as NIW 4810, while YYE 270T was loaned back to London Buses and used initially to carry aid to Romania, and was never subsequently converted to single-door. The remainder were converted from 36-seat dual door vehicles to single-door with seating for 44, and one received a DAF engine, whilst twelve were fitted with Volvo units. Further Leyland Nationals from London Buses were nine Series-2 models acquired in 1994 towards the end of operations. Series-1 Volvo-powered National BYW 367V is seen negotiating the bend on Station Hill in Bargoed on 23 March 1995. Just over a week later, on 1 April 1995 Parfitt's sold their bus services to Rhondda Buses, which brought to an end a popular and well respected operator. At the end of operations the fleet comprised thirty-four buses, including four Dennis Darts, three of which had been purchased new in 1994. Leyland National BYW 367V along with ten other Parfitt's Nationals were to see further service with Liverline on Merseyside from May 1995, passing to North Western two months later.

(John Wiltshire)

Having become a subsidiary of Stagecoach Holdings plc in December 1993, the Red and White fleet rapidly gained the corporate white livery with red, blue and orange stripes. The first new group vehicles allocated to the Red and White fleet arrived in early 1994 and consisted of seventeen Mercedes-Benz 709D minibuses and a dozen Volvo B6 saloons, all with Alexander bodywork. The B6 model was Volvo's answer to the Dennis Dart, and the Stagecoach group took a large number around this time. However as already mentioned it was not particularly successful. The Stagecoach Red and White batch had 40-seat bodies to the Dash styling, and was based at Merthyr Tydfil. This view is of a rather smartly turned out number 704 (L704 FWO), which has just arrived at the entrance to Merthyr's bus station on 29 March 1995. From 15 May 1995, the services in Merthyr previously run in competition with Red and White, and acquired by Rhondda Buses from Parfitt's Motor Services the previous month, passed to Red and White. Only Pontsticill and some evening services were retained by Rhondda Buses, and from now on, Stagecoach would be the dominant operator in Merthyr Tydfil. By 2000 four of the twelve Volvo B6s batch had been transferred away to another Stagecoach fleet, and none would survive very much longer with Stagecoach.

(Andrew Wiltshire)

Cardiff Bluebird ran an interesting mixture of Leyland Atlanteans as well as four former London DMS-type Fleetlines. These buses formed the backbone on a network of services which gradually expanded across Cardiff during 1994, and took in new destinations such as Llanrumney and St Mellons. The next type of double-decker to arrive was the MCW Metrobus, and initially three slightly more unusual Alexander-bodied examples were purchased. Two of these came from Black Prince of Morley in November 1994, and were originally new to West Yorkshire PTE. The third example was number 72 (ULS 621X), a former Midland Scottish bus, that had arrived from Capital Citybus in January 1995 and is seen on Kingsway in the centre of Cardiff on 12 April 1995. It is inbound from Llanrumney and passing the old Prudential Building which in 2012 is the Cardiff Hilton hotel. Five further Metrobuses added to the fleet in 1995 were of the more conventional MCW-bodied variety that had been new to South Yorkshire PTE. The subject of this view would gain further notoriety when it became an open-top bus serving amongst other places the city of Norwich.

(Andrew Wiltshire)

Following the very successful operation of a varied fleet of Leyland Leopard saloons, Glyn Williams of Crosskeys went on to build up a sizeable fleet of Leyland Nationals. By July 1991, vehicles were operating out of premises at Pennar Halt garage at Pentwynmawr near Pontllanfraith, having outgrown the yard in Crosskeys, which was later sold. The first Leyland National arrived in 1990 and was the first of several former National Welsh buses, and coincided with a change in fleet livery to green and white. Further examples came from a wide variety of sources, and included some former London examples from Cyril Evans. RBO 24R came from National Welsh in 1991 and was one of the buses acquired from Taff-Ely in September 1988 when that fleet sold out. Fleet numbers have always been allocated to the service bus fleet and RBO 24R became number 3. It is seen on 2 September 1995 in Blackwood making the final ascent to the bus station which is located on the hillside to the west of the main street. Glyn Williams went on to operate a small fleet of Leyland National 2s before embarking upon a policy of buying new Mercedes-Benz minibuses from 1994, and the first of a large fleet of Dennis Darts from 1997 onwards. Glyn Williams continued operating stage services until 2006 when he sold out to Stagecoach South Wales.

(John Jones)

In 1992, the year that witnessed the demise of National Welsh, an employee buy-out of operations at the Bedwas depot was destined to fail, and the Caerphilly Buslink services based at this site ceased to run after 16 February. Subsequently, a smaller scale operation was established by the same consortium that had acquired Porth depot, and still based in Waddon's yard. When the new company, Rhondda Bus Ltd was set up with its own operator licence, Bedwas once again began trading, this time as Caerphilly Busways. The early fleet consisted of MCW Metroriders (some of which had been new to Inter Valley Link), together with a handful of Leyland Nationals and Ford Transits. In May 1993 the services of Cyril Evans were acquired together with some vehicles, and at this time a revised livery of red, cream and maroon similar to that used by Cyril Evans was adopted for the Caerphilly unit. In June 1995, a new Bedwas depot was opened for the exclusive use of the fleet owned by Rhondda Bus. The previous year the first new vehicles were added to the Caerphilly Busways fleet, including five Plaxton-bodied Volvo B6s, and a pair of 9-metre Dennis Darts with 34-seat Marshall bodywork. One of the latter, number 68 (M68 HHB), is seen in Castle Street, Caerphilly on 15 September 1995 on one of several routes to Senghenydd.

(John Jones)

Phil Anslow Travel's N417 UWN is seen on 26 April 1996 outside the Settlement Education Centre in Pontypool, and was one of an increasing number of new minibuses to join the fleet from 1993. N417 UWN was a 29-seat UVG-bodied Iveco Turbo Daily dating from 1996, but Mercedes-Benz minibuses were also purchased around this time. By the early 1990s Anslow was dominant on Pontypool area services, and went on to establish some longer routes to places such as Chepstow, Newport, Blackwood and Brynmawr. The fleet was originally based at premises situated at Varteg Hill, and later a garage was established at Blaenavon. As the business expanded a large depot and yard was opened at Pontnewynydd. From about 1999 larger buses were preferred, and a number of Leyland National 2s joined the fleet. The subsequent history of Phil Anslow is interesting as in September 2000 all stage services, some contracts and 27 buses passed to Stagecoach Red and White, on the condition that he did not recommence stage work for at least two years. He did start up again in 2002 running services, but in November 2004 sold up again, with further vehicles and the Pontnewynydd depot passing to Stagecoach. By 2011 Phil Anslow was back on the scene again, and starting to build up a portfolio of services in the Blackwood, Cwmbran and Newport areas.

(John Jones)

The success of the new DAF-based Optare Delta saloons prompted Richards of Cardigan to purchase two used examples in 1992 and 1994. From 1994 onwards three further brand-new Dennis Darts were added to stock as well as a rather smart Optare Vecta saloon, which was based on the MAN 11.190 chassis and had seating for 40 passengers. This shot of the Vecta M197 CDE was taken at Haverfordwest railway station on 18 March 1996. It had worked on service 412 from Cardigan via Fishguard and was lying over prior to making a return trip. The Bedford parked alongside would be one of the buses operating the service from St Davids that day. Further additions to the Richards fleet included a pair of two-year-old Northern Counties-bodied DAF SB220s from Leeds-Bradford Airport in 1998, as well as a number of Mercedes minibuses. Continuing local authority support into the new millennium allowed passengers to benefit from additional new full-size saloons, including an Optare Excel, two impressive Optare Tempos and a number of Transbus Enviro 300s. Quality used buses would also be purchased, and in 2011 Richards Bros, in addition to operating a modern fleet of coaches, remains a major player, with its much-respected bus operations in Pembrokeshire and south Ceredigion.

(Andrew Wiltshire)

In a similar fashion to the Renault PR100 (see page 63), the Iveco Turbo City was a chassis that was introduced to the UK in the hope that it might gain some of the success it had achieved in mainland Europe. Only eight were built for service in Britain between 1991 and 1995, including one which was bodied as an 83-seat double-decker in 1991. Six of the saloons were bodied by Wadham Stringer with Vanguard II style bodywork, and two of these entered the Shamrock fleet in 1994, during their first year of service. These rear-engined buses were to have mixed fortunes, and spent long periods out of service awaiting spares, but when active could be found working into Cardiff on services such as the X6 from Aberdare. The photographer has been most fortunate to capture both of these buses in this view taken on 28 March 1996. L775 GNM is passing through Pontypridd bus station on an X6 working, while parked behind and surrounded by Mercedes minibuses is sister bus L957 JGS. Both were sold in February 2006 and before Shamrock was sold to the French-owned Veolia group. They both passed to South East Coachworks in Faversham, with L775 GNM being converted to a mobile showroom for Aurora Lighting in London.

(John Wiltshire)

Newport Transport did not operate any minibuses until after deregulation and in 1987 took delivery of eleven Dodge S56s. Eight of these had particularly ungainly East Lancs bodies, while the final trio were completed by Reeves Burgess along more attractive lines. In 1988, a pair of far more business-like MCW Metroriders was added to the fleet, and these were followed by a dozen Optare-built examples in 1990/91 which replaced the earlier Dodges. In April 1994 Newport acquired a 1987 vintage, former London Buses MCW Metrorider, D478 PON from Parfitt's Motor Services, for use solely on the Royal Gwent Hospital free bus service 99. Numbered 39, the bus was never actually fitted with fare collection equipment and so never wandered on to other duties. A similar bus D477 PON was acquired from Cardiff Bluebird in 1996 and numbered 36. On a fine 13 May 1996, number 39 complete with Newport Nipper branding, heads out of Newport bus station bound for the hospital. This bus was withdrawn in August 1997, and shortly after passed to the local fleet of Croydon Minibus Hire, Newport, and was eventually scrapped by 2003.

(John Jones)

In January 1996 Cardiff Bus surprised many when it purchased a dozen used Ailsas from Merseybus for further service. These would bolster the Ailsa fleet to forty-eight examples of this rugged and reliable model. Unlike the Northern Counties-bodied Ailsas that Cardiff had purchased new between 1982 and 1984, these would have the more recognisable (for an Ailsa), Alexander RH bodywork with 82 seats and would take fleet numbers 437 to 448. The vehicles were thoroughly refurbished and entered service over a five-month period appearing in the same livery as carried by Scanias 601 to 610. Having not long entered service we see number 438 (A152 HLV) on 20 July 1996 working service 47 from Llanrumney. It has just descended Kingsway and is turning into Duke Street, and making its way to the bus station. It is pleasingly free of advertisements apart from the two "Pick an Orange" roundels. A152 HLV, new in 1984, was originally number 0070 in the Merseyside PTE fleet, and part of a batch of fifteen bought for evaluation. It was withdrawn from service by Cardiff in May 2001 and by 2002 had become a mobile computer classroom for Cardiff City Council. In 2011 it briefly passed to Edwards of Llantwit Fardre for use as a static office, but was quickly sold without being used.

(John Jones)

In May 1995 Rhondda Bus purchased Rossendale Transport's coach-seated long-wheelbase Leyland Olympian which had a Leyland TL11 engine and became number 850 at Porth. It was not a major success but did last until August 1996. Slightly more successful double-deckers were two under-floor engined Volvo Citybus, F50/51 ACL, acquired from the erstwhile Great Yarmouth Transport fleet in June 1995. New in March 1989, they had 84-seat Alexander RV bodywork and took fleet numbers 851 and 852 at Rhondda Bus. During their time in South Wales they were regular performers into Cardiff on the 132 service from Maerdy and here we see number 852 (F51 ACL) on 10 May 1996, having disembarked passengers outside Antics model shop in High Street. Behind 852 can be seen Cardiff Bus Optare Metrorider 142. These two Volvos were sold in January 1997 to Chambers of Bures in Suffolk who, as part of the deal, sent Leyland Lynx E87 KGV to Rhondda Bus. In 2011 both vehicles remain together as a pair with Dew of Somersham in Cambridgeshire. On 23 December 1997 Rhondda Bus Ltd, including the Parfitt's Motor Services Ltd licence passed to Stagecoach Holdings. Porth depot began operating as Stagecoach Rhondda, while the Caerphilly Busways depot at Bedwas passed to Stagecoach Red and White.

(John Jones)

The last bus to enter service with Cardiff Bluebird in July 1996 was yet another MCW Metrorider, in this case E837 BTN which was given fleet number 17. It had begun life in 1988 with Northumbria, but was latterly working with another British Bus Group subsidiary, Kentish Bus. It was finished in the later Cardiff Bluebird livery which used less white, and was put to work on the hourly L3 service which served Llandough Hospital, picking up in Ely, Canton, Riverside and Grangetown. Number 17 would also appear on the Asda Free Bus Service at Pontprennau from time to time during the late summer of 1996. This interesting shot on 5 August 1996 depicts number 17 waiting at the traffic lights in Canton alongside Cardiff Bus Metrorider 109 on an Ely service. The drivers, despite working for competing operators, are taking the opportunity to have a brief chat while the traffic lights are red. At the end of operations on 7 September 1996 the Cardiff Bluebird fleet consisted of two Dennis Darts, eight Atlanteans, eight Metrobuses, fifteen MCW Metroriders, eight Dodge minibuses and a Leyland Leopard. Cardiff Bus acquired all but the two Darts, but ultimately sold all the buses without using any of them.

(Andrew Wiltshire)

From 1992 there was a marked move away from the double-decker at Newport Transport. Full-size vehicles were required to replace older double-deckers, and so in 1993 the first six of thirty Scania N113 single-deckers with Alexander Strider bodywork was delivered. They were numbered 4-9 (K104-9 YTX) and replaced a number of MCW Metrobuses. The following year a further half dozen similar buses arrived as 68-73. These were fitted with Euro 1 specification engines, had seating for 48 and entered service from February 1994. In this shot number 73 (L73 EKG) has left Newport bus station around midday on 13 August 1996, and is heading west, out to the Duffryn estate on service 15A. The road layout at this location has now completely changed and the footbridge behind the bus has long disappeared. The final Alexander Strider bodied Scanias arrived in 1997 and the last were withdrawn in 2011. As for number 73, it was withdrawn in August 2007 and would eventually see further service with B&J Travel of Barnoldswick.

(Andrew Wiltshire)

For the final three years of its existence as a major bus group, Badgerline adopted the rear-engine Dennis Lance as one of its standard single-deck models. Matched with the Plaxton Verde body, the Lance had a Cummins engine and ZF transmission, and was to be found working for Midland Red West, Yorkshire Rider and Badgerline, with early examples appearing in the South Wales Transport fleet. SWT took ten in late 1993 with seating for 45 passengers, and allocated them to Pontardawe for the "Timecutter" branded services that ran from Swansea to Neath and further afield, to places such as Glyn Neath, Banwen, Tonmawr and Porthcawl. On 27 December 1996 we see number 825 in Neath's Victoria Gardens bus station on a 158 working from Banwen to Swansea, caught by strong sunlight on a crisp winter's afternoon. By now SWT was part of First Bus Group although the bus has yet to gain First Bus logos. The batch was later transferred to Port Talbot where they would be joined by three similar former Midland Red West examples. From then on they would be put to work on the limited stop services X1 and X2, the latter taking them from Porthcawl to Bridgend and on to Cardiff using the A48. All thirteen Lances were subsequently transferred to First Midland Red in December 2003.

(John Jones)